Turning Point

A powerful step-by-step guide
to feeling better about yourself
to reach your full potential

AARON RENTFREW

Content

Aaron Rentfrew

The Pitch

"Everyone thinks of changing the world, but no one thinks of changing themselves."

—Leo Tolstoy

Congratulations on making the decision to take charge of unlocking your true potential!

There is a plethora of different diet plans and fitness programs geared to sell you guaranteed weight loss. One thing they rarely address is the personal struggle many of us deal with on a day-to-day basis. Spending money on different programs without addressing the root cause of your issue is a path to failure, frustration, and broken promises.

Luckily, there are ways to get off the hamster wheel and get motivated from deep within. In this book, we will discuss methods that are guaranteed to help you develop a newfound respect for yourself — methods that will resonate with anyone. The point is to be able to look in the mirror and say honestly for the first time, "I'm worth it" — and to mean it deep in your core and firmly believe it.

Everyone, regardless of past failures, is capable of drastic change. You can achieve the change you want if you are willing to work though the phases of the Turning Point program, which I will lay out for you here. These are proven techniques that have worked in my life and have brought me from the depths of depression to heading up companies and guiding several hundred employees using motivation and personal growth.

The sky is truly the limit when you are able get out of your own way. The most terrifying thought is that there is always a good excuse to put off until later the actions that could change your life for the better right now.

Come on this journey with me to personal growth and realize your true potential.

Locked inside you is the ability to tackle all the goals you think about every day. The Turning Point phases are designed to give a megaphone to that little voice in the back of your mind that constantly tells you, "I'm capable of so much more." Untether your inner will and get started today. You will never look at life's hurdles the same way again. Instead, you will be equipped with the tools to handle future barriers, and you will never look back!

My Story

Let me start by saying that the Turning Point program is completely about *honesty*. If you are reading this, clearly you are on the path to not only better physical health but improved mental health, as well. I believe the two are closely related.

But how could I possibly ask you to be brutally honest with yourself if I am not willing to be open and honest with you? To understand how my message can dramatically alter your way of life, it's important that you know where I come from and where I am today. And should you ever choose to pass on this gift from yourself to another person, it should always start with your personal story of triumph and the growth you went through along the way. I ask you to read my personal story not so much for the events that unfolded but to understand the emotions and feelings they generated. That is, after all, what most people will be able to recognize in their own lives.

I was born in Orlando, Florida, to two young lovers who had their entire lives ahead of them. At birth, I was missing a baby's typical "soft spot," because the bones of my skull, rather than being made up of the usual six pieces that fuse together as a child grows, were already one solid bone. As a result, as an infant, I had to undergo surgery to physically break my skull into smaller pieces so that my brain could develop properly. I was quite lucky, actually; just a few years earlier, most babies born with this condition died within a few short years.

Up until preschool, my childhood was pretty normal. My mother and father were always trying to make ends meet and doing what they could to protect me. I vaguely remember my father having season tickets for the local minor league baseball teams, so we went to a lot of games. We frequented Gatorland Zoo, Disney, and other attractions where kids typically have fun.

It was during this time that events took a turn that would alter the course of my life. After the baseball games, we would sometimes go to my father's best friend's house. (For the purposes of this story, I will call this friend "Jack.") The parents would relax and enjoy post-game cocktails while Jack's son and I would run off and "play." I was only about 3 years old at the time, and Jack's son was an early teen. While I won't go into details that might disturb some readers, suffice it to say that the end result was several months of sexual molestation that for one reason or another flew under my parents' radar. (Feel free to email me directly if you would like more information or want to share your own story.)

The issue came to light one day when we were planning to go over to Jack's house. I started crying that I didn't want to go and then just blurted out to my parents what was going on. My parents immediately scrambled to determine the best course of action. Our pediatrician recommended that the best way to proceed was to not make an issue out of it but rather to question me thoroughly about everything that had happened and to let me know that none of it was my fault. It was important that nothing be left out of my story; I was supposed to totally empty my mind. After that, the thinking was that I would feel guilt-free and "cleansed." The idea was that by letting it all out and not suppressing the memories, those memories would not linger. Given my age, that was probably the appropriate thing to do, because it actually worked for many years. It didn't pop up again in my mind until many years later.

Shortly after this episode in my life, my parents divorced. Growing up, I always felt as though the divorce was somehow my fault, but being a child, I had no real way to understand the dynamics.

After their divorce, both my parents were financially strapped. Money had been tight before, and the situation was far worse once they were on individual incomes. As a result, it was decided that it was best for me to stay with a foster family for a year. I was now in first grade, and my foster parents put me in the same school their children attended, which was a Christian academy. I never really felt a part of that family. It was a dark time for me, and I was not used to life in an extremely religious household. When we would go to the arcade at the mall, I was the child with no quarters who was relegated to watching my "brothers" play video games. It seems like a small thing now, but at the time, it left me feeling extremely alienated and alone.

Finally, after several months of tearful phone calls and copious amounts of guilt, my mother couldn't take it anymore and took me to live with her in her apartment in Texas. We had no money whatsoever — I lived on ramen noodles and spaghetti — but I was back with my mother, which was all that mattered to either of us.

For the next several years, I bounced back and forth between my parents — second grade in Texas with Mom and third and fourth grade in Orlando with Dad. At the end of fourth grade, I asked my Dad if I could live with my Mom again. For fifth grade, Mom and I moved to New Jersey, and things finally started to settle down for me as I entered adolescence. My mother met a new man — a good guy by all rights. He took me skiing, surfing, and fishing, and he taught me how to build things. The situation was finally looking up, and I made several lifelong friends. I was able to stay in one area for several years, and life was very good.

Around freshman year in high school, things began to change for me. Bad memories started to crop up, my attitude switched, and I began spiraling downward. The memories of my early childhood began to haunt me a bit, and I wasn't sure whether I was remembering real events or things that I had imagined. Vivid snapshots of childhood feelings, emotions, and actual events began to plague my mind, and nothing I could do would calm them.

Of course, there were things that would ease my mind temporarily — first pot and food, and later, other drugs and alcohol. But nothing I tried could rid me of the lingering feeling that there was something wrong with me. At the end of the day, I was constantly left feeling that I just wasn't good enough. I was incapable of feeling that I was a part of any group, my relationships were strained, and my insecurities began to bloom. This wasn't the way my life was supposed to turn out. Things were supposed to get better, and then I would sail off into the sunset with a good story — that's what I thought should have happened.

Alas, this went on for another decade. There were cycles of depression, anxiety, self-loathing, blame, and even thoughts of suicide toward the end. I was stuck in a cycle of self-pity and suffered from an overwhelming sense that I didn't belong to any particular group. There were breaks in the clouds once in a while —times when things seemed like they might get better — but then, lo and behold, resentments and fear would *always* bring me back down.

I tried several approaches to fixing the problem from the outside, but these attempts were like Band-Aids on a hatchet wound. I wound up trying to treat the symptoms of the real issue one at a time: I'd quit drinking; I'd quit drugs; I'd go to the gym; I'd try to eat better. They were all short-lived attempts and never addressed the root cause of the problem. Eventually, each one failed.

It was at this point in my life that things really started to bottom out. This time, though, something was different. I wasn't at the typical broke, depressed, false-promise-laden type of bottom. In many ways, I felt like I was at the absolute end of the road and that I couldn't go on any further. I had been defeated. There was an element of surrender, and the excuses were gone. Looking back on this time in my life feels far different than when I was in the middle of it, but one thing is for sure: The pain I was in had finally outweighed the pain it would take to change my life for the better.

I'm fully aware that life change can be painful. There is an element of comfort in the familiar that I came to appreciate in even my most beaten-down state. It was as if fear of a normal, healthy life had kept me in a stupor. Always ready with excuse after excuse for why certain things just wouldn't work for me, I was constantly looking through the window at other, happy people and wondering why I couldn't be the same.

So, let's review where I was before I set my course toward physical and mental health:

- I had been smoking since the age of 15.
- I was fat.
- I had inflammation all over my body and throughout my joints from years of being lazy.
- Heavy drinking and lack of overall care had damaged my internal organs.
- I hadn't been to a dentist in several years and had several issues with my teeth.
- I was pretty much always looking for a way to skirt any possible responsibility.

- I was never in a good mood and was more or less miserable to be around.
- I had never finished anything and resisted starting new things.
- I had no drive to move forward in my career.
- My relationships with others were poor.
- I owed money to half my family.
- I was unlovable because I hated myself.
- I was deep in debt.
- My apartment was a mess.
- I had a short temper.

The list could go on and on, but I'm sure you get the point. But here's the thing: No matter what personal issues you may have, the Turning Point system works. It's a proven method that has worked wonders in my life, and there is no doubt it can do the same for you if you are ready to be honest and are willing to put in the necessary time and effort to put yourself on the path to greatness.

Aaron Rentfrew

The Turning Point

The Workbook for these Phases can be found at the Link Below

https://livingright.co/books/download

When I had finally bottomed out emotionally, something amazing happened: I was able to let my guard down. I was now *willing* to do whatever I could to turn things around. Hopefully, that is exactly the type of thinking that has led you to this book, and that's why we are now going to delve into the business of creating self-worth and healing, which will forever change the way you look at your problems. Let's look at what I call the "turning point," so we can begin to understand the power of breaking down walls and cleaning up the past.

I would love to say that change happened overnight for me, but that wouldn't be accurate. There were stumbles along the way, things didn't always turn out as I had planned, and there were times that I wanted to say, "Fuck it!" as I had many times before.

However, as I mentioned in my story, something was different now, and that glaring thing was *honesty*. I knew deep down in my core that I could no longer keep telling myself that I wasn't worthy. That was the moment that Phase 1 began for me. As we go along here, I will share my experiences with each phase.

But before we move forward, allow me to tell you about my life today. These days, I can look at myself in the mirror and be proud of my growth as a person. I have an amazing relationship with both my parents. I have successfully managed businesses with more than 200 employees under my direct supervision and created an environment of honesty, respect, and accountability — something I never would have thought I could do. I have personally developed leaders in my field of expertise and pushed them forward with positive energy and a solid moral compass. People come to me for help on a regular basis, and providing that help is a source of strength for me.

In the six years since I completed the program you are about to commence, I have never compromised my personal set of core values. People who know me trust me with their lives. I have zero debt. Through it all, I've been able to carry a message of hope and change to those around me who are willing to listen and take action. I now live a life that I never would have thought was possible — and I do it by turning my problems inside out. You will surely get a far greater reward out of this process than you can possibly imagine if you are only willing to do what it requires.

At the core of this system is one undeniable truth: If you cannot be honest with yourself about who and what you are, you should shut this book and try something different.

How the Program Works

This type of program has been tested by millions of people with thousands of different ailments, and it all boils down to what an individual is willing to do. I highly recommend that once you begin the phases, you work them through as quickly as possible. Procrastination will keep you from getting through the tough work of change. It is no secret that change is painful, and if you're not ready for it, you will surely find an excuse to put it off for another day.

Let's start from the beginning: Phase 1. It is very important that you go through all the phases in order and that you complete them thoroughly. Although there are only four phases, it could take several days or weeks to get to Phase 4. As I said earlier, the business of change is not simple, and it's by all rights an inside job. Fixing yourself from within in order to accomplish your goals is a rigorous task, but if you're ready to do it, let's go!

Phase 1 – Getting Honest

Overview

Getting honest seems simple enough, right? Wrong! For some people, this phase is one of the toughest, and that's why it's first. For me, getting truly honest with myself was one of the toughest tasks I had ever undertaken. But if you've made it this far, you are clearly ready, willing, and open to getting the job done.

Remember, at this point in the process, you are only dealing with yourself. This is about an honest reflection of who you are, where you have come from, and where you would like to be — nothing more and nothing less. It's a no-holds-barred level of introspection that will be followed by a plan to put your goals into action. But first, you must start by identifying those things that made you fall short in the past.

Start off by listing all of your past failures, omitting nothing and being brutally honest about things in the past for which you may have laid the blame elsewhere. Here are some of the typical scapegoats people use for their own failures:

- Emotions
- Physical limitations
- Fear
- Financial insecurity
- Too hard
- Too easy
- Spouses
- Peer pressure
- Parents
- Other people

This list could go on ad infinitum, but the point is to recognize your failures for what they are, and the first step in this process is to let your guard down about these things and come clean. It's time to call a spade a spade and get to work on the business of personal growth, and that starts with taking personal responsibility.

Phase 1 includes a worksheet where you can begin to identify these incidents, their causes, the effects, and the underlying reasons that you haven't yet reached your own turning point.

Honesty Is the Key

Repeat after me: "The person I was before will always make the same mistakes."

Accomplishing true, lasting change requires seeing yourself clearly. It's time to hold nothing back as you strip away the dense shell within which you have wrapped your true self. This process cannot be completed unless you are absolutely, brutally honest to your innermost self about the true nature of your past.

Most of us tend to move through life achieving some minor successes here and there. As we go, our minds are constantly craving something more — some societal ideal of what we think we are supposed to be. More often than not, our current reality overrules such thought, and we stagnate and justify our positions. It's a circular problem that we resolve by taking no action at all. But as the old saying goes, if you want to make an omelet you have to break a few eggs. In this case, the eggs are our fears and the omelet is our goals.

Imagine a world where we were all unencumbered by fear, doubt, insecurity, and regrets. Can you embrace the philosophy that we only get one shot at life, and none of us gets out alive? If you are riding the crest and living at the pinnacle, then I applaud you, but if you are anything like me, that type of feeling takes a great deal of effort. It takes a deep and accurate appraisal of the assets and liabilities of your thought processes. To generate great change, you must get down to the nuts and bolts that underlie your decision-making process.

We all have our own experiences and individual struggles, but with the billions of different possible scenarios, there are but a handful of feelings that people experience as a result. Put very simply, you can look at the way your past has made you feel — both then and now — and begin to break down the barriers that are stunting your growth.

You may be asking yourself, "What does all this have to do with the fact that I haven't stuck to my diet/fitness program/relationships?" My answer to that is simple: Everything! The emotions that drive us to give up are fear and doubt. The Turning Point process is designed to teach you how to turn fear and doubt upside down — to look your issues directly in the eye and understand that these emotions are just illusions meant to guard you from the pain of change.

If you don't believe me, take a walk into the bathroom and just stare at yourself in the mirror for a few minutes. Tell yourself, "I've never quit because of fear or doubt, I've never quit because of what other people might think, and I've never quit because I feared what change would bring." If you can honestly look at yourself and say these things, then you probably don't need this book. For the rest of us, these are real issues that keep us from our true potential. For me, these fears were so great that I wouldn't even get started on anything, much less quit.

In Practice

This is where the work begins. This is, after all, a program built around action. To believe that simply reading a book could potentially change your life in the long term is wishful thinking. I've read plenty of self-help books meant to help me take charge of my life, yet a week after finishing one, someone would honk at me in traffic and I'd lose my mind.

Truth and action are the keys to moving forward in this process. It will not be easy, but it will be worth it. You are going to take yourself apart and put yourself back together in a meaningful way. Anyone who tells you that there's a way you can do that without action is selling you snake oil — save your money.

I highly recommend that you don't skip forward in this book; it's not a race. There is no prize for sprinting to the finish line; rather, you will have won the true prize if, at the end of all four phases, you can look back and say you left nothing hiding under the surface. This is about shining the sunlight on things you have kept "safe" and in the dark. There is no time limit, but you should resist the urge to procrastinate. Remember, change is always difficult. Your mind is going to tell you that you should give up on this; nothing else has worked, so why should this? Push through the doubt and finish this book and the process. You'll thank me at the end.

Phase 1 is about prior goals. The purpose of this phase is to list and break down every element of the past that you can think of concerning your goals — specifically your unfinished goals.

Goals can be disguised as other things, as well — promises you made to yourself or others, deadlines, milestones, and childhood dreams that never came to fruition. Put it all on paper — every little thing you can think of that is still somewhere in your mind as an unfinished sentence and anything left uncompleted that you had always intended to finish. It doesn't matter what the circumstances were surrounding the goal; what matters for this step is putting pen to paper and writing down the past.

Leave no stone unturned.

Start by filling out the chart and then reviewing it. Remember, at this point, we are stripping away any guilt or blame related to these prior goals and just making a point-blank appraisal of what happened. Keep your emotions out of this exercise, and focus on the facts surrounding these times in your life. You may want to put this in a journal so that you have more space to elaborate for yourself.

After reading the instructions below, put down this book and get started with the Phase 1 workbook . Once you have fully completed it to the absolute best of your ability, you should take a day to reflect on it and then move on to Phase 2.

Instructions for Completing the Phase 1 Exercise

Goal: List every goal that you have ever really wanted to achieve but did not. Go back as far as you can remember, and leave nothing out. When I went through this exercise, I needed several of these charts, so feel free to make copies if necessary.

Result: How long did you work toward this goal? How did it end? Did it fizzle out or end spectacularly?

Excuse: What was the primary justification you used for not completing this goal at the time you abandoned it?

Real Reason: Looking back on it now, what was the real reason you did not achieve this goal?

How You Felt After: When you gave up on your goal, were you relieved, ashamed, guilty, or remorseful? Be honest!

Still a Goal of Yours? A simple "yes" or "no" will do here.

The Workbook for this Phase can be found at the Link Below https://livingright.co/books/download

Phase 2 – Taking Stock

Overview

In Phase 1, we were simply building a list of past behaviors and trying to identify the effect. While that practice can be eye-opening, it can also be painful to relive the past. Hopefully, if you gained anything from Phase 1, it was the power of the truth. It is often said, "The truth shall set you free," and nowhere is that more true than when you are digging in and working on personal growth from the inside. If you're incapable of the truth in an introspective practice, then personal growth and goal achievement will continue to remain just out of your reach. Put simply, if you cannot be truthful to yourself, you will never gain anything from this process.

While it is loosely related to Phase 1, Phase 2 will bring you to the root causes of your present and past behavior. Our life experiences shape us as humans, but rarely do we stop to look at how certain life experiences may have changed us for the better or the worse.

Let me share my own experiences with Phase 2 to help you understand how it works.

Background

When I had finally given up and was at an emotional bottom, I was truly down and out. I had completely given up; everything I tried in an effort to push forward would quickly fail or be put back on the shelf for the next idea. I was out of shape, broke, always negative, always blaming others, and incapable of looking at myself in the mirror.

Why did I feel this way? I was not a bad person. I genuinely wanted to be better, but no matter what, I couldn't shake these negative feelings. I knew that I had issues in my past that I was avoiding, but I had never really bothered to consider that my current feelings and behavior were possibly being shaped by events long past. I had built up walls of resentments, and unspoken fears were eating away at me bit by bit.

When I was finally ready, I laid out a course of action that I could live with. I began with an internal quest. I started from my earliest memories and worked forward in time. I wrote down everything I could remember — every trauma, every resentment, every fear, and every time I felt cheated, sold short, or ripped off. I had two lists: on one, people who had wronged me, and on the other, people I had harmed. The people whom I had affected most were family, but there were others whom I had hurt via neglect, dishonesty, stress, sex, loans, and general erratic behavior.

Once I had this master list of my personal low points, I felt like I was getting somewhere. So now, it was imperative to see how these things affected me. Did they make me feel fearful, angry, isolated, or inferior? What emotion did I feel at the time, and how did it feel now? If I saw these people on the street, would I look them in the eyes and say hello, or would I hide and try to avoid them? I literally wrote out everything associated with these events that I thought might help me find the answer.

But how do you find the answer if you don't even know the question? I wanted to identify the thing or situation that had brought me down the path of self-destruction and failure. Would I even know if the answer was staring me straight in the face? These are the questions I would typically ask myself as I considered giving up. But I pushed through the process. Regardless of the outcome, I knew I had a plan, and if I never stuck to anything else in my life, I was going to finish this one thing.

In Practice

When I went through this process, I divided all the hurts and wrongs I could remember into two categories: "Hurt Me" and "Hurt Others." Additionally, I added a list labeled "Fears." I then subdivided each list into categories that included fears, resentments, sex issues, financial issues, family, and friends.

On the worksheet, you'll see checkboxes for the topics "Pride," "Security," and "Relationships." Just check the box when it applies. If you check a box, then follow up by filling in the section labeled "My Part." Do your best to fill in all this information. In certain instances, you may not think you had a part at first glance — say, for example, if someone stole your identity or robbed your house. But if you feel that you had any part in any of the listed items, be sure to note it.

For me, making these lists was rather tedious because I had so many items to include. For others with whom I've worked, the lists have been much shorter. What matters here is that you leave nothing out. Put it *all* down. After all, what do you have to lose by getting truthful with yourself?

Once I had the issues in front of me to look at, things became very clear, and you will find that in Phase 3, this truthful, in-depth inventory of yourself will come to life. But for now, the key is to just fill in the blanks, leaving nothing out. You may or may not use all the spaces; the worksheet is just a guide. In fact, I highly recommend using a notebook rather than the worksheet itself, so you can devote as much attention as needed to certain areas of your life while putting less effort into those that don't merit as much focus.

In the sample worksheet, I have filled in some of my actual issues in each category, so you can get an idea of what the process looks like before filling out your own.

Truth Is the Key

Keep in mind that at this point, we are simply putting pen to paper. You will get out of this practice whatever you put into it, so the more thorough you are, the bigger the payoff will be at the end. There is no point in letting something linger hidden in the annals of your mind. Get it all out, set the record straight, and let the truth flow freely.

We *all* have some hurts hiding, and hopefully you will find them. I talk to people all the time who tell me they've never harmed anyone, and I just have to laugh. Have you never tried to discredit someone else's beliefs or work? Have you never insulted someone? Have you never withheld your love from someone who cared about you? Have you never screamed at a clerk or teller for something that person couldn't control? The list of ways you can hurt someone could go on forever, because other people have feelings just like you do!

I highly recommend that you do not start reading about the next phase until you have completed this phase to the best of your ability, based on your best memory of past events.

This is not just about people; in addition to all the individuals you may have hurt or who have hurt you, you should list any institutions that you may have affected or that have affected you in some negative way. Debtors, creditors, churches, and businesses — no one gets a pass here. This exercise may take some time, but make progress every day and push through until you have completed the task.

Be fearless in this practice. There doesn't need to be a lot on your lists, but you do need to include everything you can think of. Leave nothing to chance, and again, leave no stone in your mind unturned.

Phase 3 – Filling the Void

Overview

If you've made it this far, then you've come a long way! You've now constructed a full slate of issues to attack that are at the root of how you feel about yourself — the issues that have shaped your decision-making for most of your life.

By now, you are surely coming to the conclusion that this is not your average self-help book. This is a design for dealing with your issues. In the coming pages, you will begin to take these issues apart and put them back together in an effort to transfer the power away from your circumstances and into your own hands.

Now is not the time for procrastination. Surely there are old wounds that have been reopened as a result of your work in the previous phases. It's important to now take the time and effort to understand all that you have on paper before you. This is a program of action. Each phase puts the onus on you to work for change. The words on paper alone will not drive true change in your life.

Action, acceptance, and enthusiasm will be the key factors from now on.

Having pulled out the bad, you must now look it in the face and change it. Of course, it's impossible to change the past, but it's very possible to change the way you view the past. Doing so is easier said than done, but with a little work and enthusiasm, you can do it.

So let's get to it!

In Practice

Phase 3 is all about digging into Phase 2. It's about reshaping your thoughts about what's happened in your past. It's about growth. It's the single most important piece to bulldozing through your fears and doubts and then building a foundation for success.

Take out your Phase 2 worksheet, so you can begin building your program of action. First, you'll attack the instances where you were hurt and your fears. Let's look at each category.

The Workbook for this Phase can be found at
the Link Below
https://livingright.co/books/download

Resentments

Someone once said to me, "Holding onto a resentment is like drinking poison and hoping the other person dies." I've never heard truer words on this topic.

Most people find that resentments are the single most difficult thing to get through, and I was no exception. One of my biggest resentments had to do with the teenager who molested me when I was a child. My anger felt so justified that I couldn't imagine how I might ever get rid of it. The mere thought of it brought about a visceral reaction that ruined me from the inside. Indeed, it was like poison. Eventually, I realized that I simply had to let go of my resentment or I would never recover from my hopeless state.

I tried many things to shake my resentment over the years, but they were mere sandbags in the path of a raging river. Today, I'm on the other side of this resentment, and I have the opportunity to help others with similar issues get through their own personal struggles. How did I do it? I used a simple four-part process for almost everything on my list:

- Get truthful.
- Open it up.
- Expose it.
- Help someone else.

That's it. What does it all mean? Let's go into a little more depth.

As I mentioned earlier, it's vital to find a way to rid ourselves of resentments. It's easy to say, "Forgive and forget," but if it were as easy to do as it is to say, you wouldn't be here right now.

We have already gotten truthful and opened it up. So now, let's examine the issues at hand and start to make sense of them. Some may be deep-seated issues. I recommend starting with those first; after dealing with them, the rest will come easily. Saving the difficult ones for last will just keep them on your mind longer, making it more likely that you will hang onto them rather than dealing with them.

How do we "expose it"? Great question! For most people, anticipating this is the toughest part. But once it begins — once you feel the freeing grace that comes with exposing the issues you have been holding onto for so long — you will never look back.

There are several different ways you can do this. No one way is right for everyone, but I have listed my personal recommendations in order of what seems to work best for the most people. I recommend the forum first because it not only allows you to share your story with other likeminded people who are trying to deal with their issues, but it gives you the opportunity to help others, as well, which will come in handy in Phase 4. Additionally, I am on the forum to give feedback quite often!

1. Visit the Turning Point forum, which is a private online forum hosted on a secure server for the exclusive use of those who have purchased The Turning Point. This forum is completely anonymous.
2. If you are working through The Turning Point with a friend, the two of you can do this phase together!
3. Go to confession at your church, if you're comfortable there.
4. Talk to a trusted friend who is supportive and totally trustworthy.
5. Choose your own adventure. By this, I mean choose someone at random. Please note that I don't recommend sharing this phase with a spouse, as this needs to be a judgment-free exercise. Instead, I recommend sharing with a complete stranger who you'll never see again over a boyfriend, girlfriend, partner, or spouse. There is no reason to open yourself up to having things used against you later.

Here's how to expose it:

Whatever canvas you wish to use to paint your story, leave nothing out. Paint the full, truthful picture. This is not about making yourself feel like a victim; it *is* about taking the power out of the resentments that have ruled you. Be sure to share your part in whatever instances are on your list, even if your biggest part is just the fact that you're still hanging onto the matter at all.

When opening up with these types of things, it's important that the person to whom you are talking to is open and likeminded — and definitely *not* one of the people to whom you harbor a resentment! You will get the most out of this phase if you're able to work on it with someone who is suffering from similar problems. When you are comfortable, you should hold nothing back; leaving things out will only hurt you in the long run. Whatever path you choose for this phase, it's important to be sure that you will be comfortable sharing everything. This is an excellent reason to do your sharing anonymously through the private Turning Point forum. You can always start there, get advice, and then try another avenue once you are more comfortable delivering your message.

What matters here is that you complete this phase. Leaving this task undone will make it all but impossible to move beyond your issues from the past. You *must* shine the light on them, see them through someone else's eyes, and grow through the experience.

It may sound like a tall order, but keep in mind that growth happens down in the valleys, not at the mountaintop. If you were to stockpile trash in your house for a long period of time, you would need to eventually take it out or there would be no room to walk around, right? The same logic applies here. Your problems, resentments, and fears are the garbage that is cluttering your mind and affecting the way you make decisions. It's high time to take the accumulated trash out for good. After that, daily maintenance becomes much easier.

You should go through your list point by point, thoroughly and honestly. More often than not, whomever you have chosen to share with during this phase will reciprocate with instances from his or her past. This person will appreciate and respect your candor as it relates to his or her own issues.

You will immediately experience an overwhelming sense of relief when this phase is completed. Your path forward will be vivid and clear, and you will feel a new sense of power. Tap into that power to get through the remainder of this program. Remember, you want this to stick for good, and for that to happen, there are some other issues you will need to resolve.

Fears

In addition to sharing your resentments, you will also share your fears in Phase 3. There is absolutely no better way to deal with fear than head on. You'll use the same process that you used for your resentments — in fact, you'll repeat this process for each category of items in this phase:

- Get truthful.
- Open it up.
- Expose it.
- Help someone else.

Given that I've never met anyone without fears, I'm going to assume that everyone has something to address here. So let's get started.

"If you want to conquer fear, don't sit home and think about it. Go out and get busy."

—Dale Carnegie

Carnegie's quote can be taken a few different ways. To many, it means to get out and do what you fear the most. That's a fair assessment of the words. But in reality, fears can sometimes paralyze us, affecting our decision-making and forcing us to avoid addressing the actual fear.

So how do we get through it? Well, to me, the "get busy" part of Carnegie's quote means addressing the reasons behind fears. For simplicity's sake, let's not get into a discussion about "healthy" versus "unhealthy" fears; rather, let's focus on things that you see other people doing freely and would love to do yourself if not for your fear — for instance, skydiving, love, public speaking, commitment, relating to people, paying bills, answering mail, or just being good enough. The list could go on and on.

The point is, there are reasons for your fears, and you must address these reasons in order to alleviate the stress associated with meeting your fears head-on.

Let's start by taking one fear and really breaking it down. Is there something that happened in your past that closely relates to your fear?

For me, my parents' divorce while I was still quite young had a profound effect on the way many of my relationships turned out. Neither of my parents remarried while I was still living at home. I was very fearful of opening up to anyone, as I had never seen a healthy adult relationship up close. I had no idea what a such a relationship looked like! I didn't even recognize this as a fear until I finally was able to get truthful and dig it out.

In search of answers, I went straight to the source on this one and spoke to my parents as well as to people who had seemingly good marriages. What seemed like a paralyzing fear was really just a matter of reorganizing the facts of the situation. My parents were just not right for one another! My fear of the unknown was all it took for me to give up and let the small voice in my head say, "Relationships never work."

All fears can be addressed in a similar manner, provided you are ready to get truthful with yourself and open about the true nature of each fear. For each one, you must find the factors that got the fear started in the first place. We were each a blank slate at one point; our fears are honed by our experiences and can be addressed by working through those experiences. But it takes action and sometimes even teamwork to get through them. (We'll talk more about teamwork in Phase 4.)

When you share your fears alongside your resentments in Phase 3 and then find the root causes of those fears, you'll be ready to start the next step, which we'll get to in Phase 4.

Financial Issues

Having issues related to money is incredibly common, especially in today's roller-coaster economy. So it's a good idea to explore the details of your own financial issues and see how you can resolve them so that they don't trouble you. Some people have too little money, some have too much, and some owe everybody in town.

What is most important here, just as in the other steps, is that you take a long look at your financial issues. The reason they are so important is that they tend to affect almost everything we touch. They are a root cause of intense stress for most people. So it's essential to categorize these issues in a way that makes sense for your life. Here's how I categorized my own financial issues, in order, from most stressful to least:

- I owed money to friends and family.
- I wasn't making enough money at work.

- Everyone else had more money than me.
- I had credit card bills.
- I had delinquent accounts.
- I had student loans.

Once you put these issues in order of what is most important to get off your shoulders first, you *must* take some action. I'm *not* saying you need to empty your bank accounts and pay everything at once — that would cause even more financial stress! What I *am* saying is that you can address these issues in order by first reaching out to the people close to you to whom you owe money.

If you're anything like me, you have avoided these issues, but they don't just go away. Sometimes, people stop asking for what they are owed, and you may lose touch with someone because of the money or item that was lent and never returned, but that doesn't mean it didn't happen. If you are going to get honest and open about the situation, you should reach out to these people even if you can't afford to pay them back. Let them know that you are aware of the debt and that you plan to make paying them back a priority. That's all that most people want to hear. Perhaps they will harbor some resentment over the issue, or they may not even want the money back at this point, but that shouldn't stop you from reaching out and trying.

This is about cleaning your side of the street; remember that. This is not about you calling everyone who owes *you* money; this is about getting out from under all the things that are holding you back from achieving your goals.

Move through your list of financial issues one step at a time. Most creditors will work with you as long as you are open with them. Tell them how much you can afford to pay — even if it's only $20 a month. But deal with it head-on. Once all these issues are addressed, you will feel like you are taking things on in a whole new way. What's important here is taking action, taking responsibility, and moving forward.

Cleaning Your Side of the Street

By this point, I'm sure you have come to the conclusion that, invariably, you will need to clear up any outstanding problems that you have left open-ended. We are now going to address the list of people you have harmed, which you created in Phase 2. It's worth noting ahead of time that you should not just run out and tell everyone on the list that you're sorry. It's important to take more care with these issues, and it's essential to do it unselfishly, with consideration for the other person's position and emotions being your top priority.

Because every situation is different, it's very important to go over this list *before* actually trying to deal with it. I highly recommend bouncing the truthful story and reasoning behind each name on the list off others in the private Turning Point forum, so you can get some helpful advice from others who have been in your shoes. Randomly going up to someone and trying to apologize for detrimental things you may have done in the past is a sure way to run into trouble. Perhaps the person has moved on. Perhaps your ex is now happily in a new relationship. It's even possible that the person you approach could turn violent.

Let's go through a few scenarios and look at how to attack these matters appropriately. There are countless possible ways that you could have hurt someone, so let's take a look at a few different categories that may apply.

Sex- or Relationship-Related

Let's be clear that this category does not include someone you propositioned for a threesome who shot you down. This category is reserved for people with whom you have had sexual relations in the past.

The most common response I get when walking others through these phases is that they want to reach out to their exes as soon as humanly possible. This is a huge mistake, because in most cases, if you are truthful with yourself, you'll realize that you are just trying to regain something that you lost, and that's selfish. When it comes to people you have harmed, contacting past romantic partners should nearly always be done dead last when it comes to cleaning up your side of the street. The only reason I have it listed first is because everyone wants to do it right away.

Once you have shared your particular issue with someone — preferably on the forum, where others will share their experiences in return — you will need to decide if it is necessary to make these amends directly with the person you have harmed or if you can instead make living amends, which means making a commitment to living your life differently so as not to make the same kinds of mistakes that harmed other people in the past.

Infidelity

There are times where making a life change can be your apology to someone. Let's say, for example, that you cheated on your current spouse. If your spouse doesn't know about it, you may do some real damage by outing the affair. In cases such as this, I recommend doing some real soul-searching in order to understand why you were unfaithful in the first place. Was it because of a lack of attention? Were you acting out? Was it an impulsive action that made you feel better about yourself? It's vital that you understand why it happened.

When I faced this issue myself, I wrote out a lengthy apology in a notebook. I made sure to include every detail, own my part in it, and admit fault. Then, I sat with it and thought about it. Finally, I brought the notebook to a park, read it one last time, and shredded the pages into the trash. I felt relieved to finally get honest about the situation and all that it entailed, and I have never looked back. If I had handled it another way, I could have really hurt someone else for selfish reasons. I strongly feel that all incidents of infidelity should be handled this way if you intend to keep your relationship together. Even if you don't intend to continue in the relationship, these incidents shouldn't be used as ammunition.

If you are no longer in the relationship and your former partner is aware of the infidelity, then perhaps a written or direct apology is in order, provided that it doesn't interfere with the other person's current relationship and that you are not looking to rekindle your past relationship with the apology. But typically, an honest appraisal of the facts of the case to your innermost self will do, especially when paired with a truthful desire to not make the same mistake again. Otherwise, these things can live with you and haunt you forever.

Other Matters

Now that we've talked about infidelity, which is very sticky and tricky, we can address other matters. Most of these can be handled in a far simpler manner: directly and truthfully.

How else would you handle a situation where you had harmed someone? There is really no other way to clean your side of the street. You've got to own up to what you did and apologize. You want to get better, right? You want to be able to look in the mirror and know that you're 100 percent worth achieving the goals you desire.

Consider each matter individually and then list them all in order, from those that will be easiest to apologize for to those where the apologies will be hardest to make. We *all* have matters like these hiding, and hopefully you've found them all. No matter how big or small each one is, this is your chance to make it right.

Start with the first name on your list — the easiest apology to make — and waste no time in doing it. After all, by this point, you should have already shed light on all of the items on your list; that's what you did at the beginning of Phase 3. By now, you should have gotten some advice on each issue and understand the intricacies involved. Additionally, should think about how you would feel if the shoe were on the other foot. How would you like someone to approach you with an apology? These are important things to consider as you prepare to make your first apology.

Here's what the other person wants to know:

- That you understand what you did wrong (your part)
- That you're not going to make the same mistake again
- That you appreciate the person enough to make a sincere apology

It's as simple as that. If the other person doesn't want to hear your apology, that's OK. What matters is that you make the attempt. This is about feeling better because you don't have skeletons in your closet or unresolved problems. You will immediately reap the benefits of being able to walk around with your head held high. You will be able to look yourself in the mirror knowing full well that your side of the street is clean and that no one can ever take that away from you.

Once this phase is complete, you will think differently about how you treat others. You'll have a new standard by which to judge your future actions. If future issues crop up, you should handle them in a similar way — right away. When you recognize that you have hurt someone, you should immediately follow the steps outlined earlier to bring the situation back into balance.

Over time, as you practice this model, your attitude toward others will change — as will your behavior. If you hold yourself to this standard over the long haul, you will naturally become more supportive and understanding of the people around you. Never forget this simple recipe for growth when you encounter future problems. It's a plan that will keep you living the life you always wanted, knowing that you're worth it. Repeat it with me, one more time:

- Get truthful.
- Open it up.
- Expose it.
- Help someone else.

The Workbook for this Phase can be found at the Link Below
https://livingright.co/books/download

Phase 4 – Giving It Away

Overview

Here we are at Phase 4, the final phase of development that will set you free from your past and help you reclaim your inner strength. "Happiness is an inside job" is the party line, but rarely does anyone give you a guide on how to get there. In this phase, we will discuss the foundation for change in your life and attitude. The steppingstones toward personal freedom and inner satisfaction are now so close, you can taste them. But how can you put what you've learned about yourself to work? It's very simple, actually.

Help Someone Else!

Every one of us is fighting a battle that others know nothing about. Equipped with the new tools you have to deal with your past, you now possess the valuable ability to help others with the same issues. If you have successfully cleaned up your side of the street to the best of your abilities, it is your duty to share that experience and help others grow in a similar manner. Having completed Phases 1 to 3, you possess valuable information about how to begin the process of self-betterment and self-understanding. Each one of us has a story unlike anyone else's, but together we can learn from one another and help each other grow with very little effort.

Thanks to the Internet, this is now possible 24 hours a day, seven days a week. The Turning Point private forum is a great place to find likeminded people sharing stories from their past. There, you can share your similar experiences and support others.

This whole process should be circular. Remember how back in Phases 2 and 3, I asked you to share your stories on the forum for advice and support? Well, now it's time to pay that back by helping and supporting others who are fighting the same battle you were waging earlier.

You would be amazed how a little encouragement and direction can dramatically help others when they know it is coming from someone who has walked a similar path and dealt with a similar situation. Rarely do people listen to blind advice, because without the benefit of a similar experience, the message doesn't carry the same weight.

When helping others, you should put yourself out there and explain how you worked through your own issues; this will help others relate to you. I'll share a few simple guidelines for this process in the In Practice section of Phase 4, but first, let me share my own experience in this process with you.

My Experience

I had gone through a tremendous amount of growth by the time I got to the point of actually giving back by sharing my experiences to help others. I had moved my career forward after working through the process I laid out in Phases 1 to 3, and I was aggressively pursuing my goals for the future. I had made great strides in my efforts to be better than I was before. I was moderately happy and had started to stagnate a bit in my career, or at least that's how I felt. I got the sense that my growth was over and that I might have exhausted the path I was on. I had cleaned up my side of the street and identified all of my past issues, so they no longer controlled my current behavior, but something was missing.

Then it happened. On an ordinary day, I experienced an epiphany that has never left my mind. I've changed my friend's name in this story to protect her privacy.

For awhile, it had become common for people to come to me with issues both small and large. They often confided in me because I'm easy to talk to and I don't repeat what others tell me. But on this day, I got served a real eye-opener. I noticed that my friend Karen was acting a bit out of sorts, which was out of character for her. I felt the need to approach her, and I am eternally grateful that I did.

I asked Karen to meet up with me for a chat. When she came in, we sat down, and I just opened up to her a little. I let her know that she was one of my favorite people, but that I had noticed that something seemed different about her. I asked whether everything was OK. She immediately started to cry, and I was a little taken aback. But I did not react; I simply looked at her and asked if she wanted my help with anything. She said yes, so I let her tell me what had happened. As it turned out, she had been raped a few days earlier and had been holding it in. Inwardly, I was very mad at whoever would do such a thing, but outwardly I stayed very calm. What happened next is the fundamental piece that you can gain through this process.

When Karen had finally gotten through telling me the details of what had happened, I asked her if I could share with her a story from my past. I went into detail about my experience of childhood sexual abuse. I explained how it controlled my life and actions all throughout early adulthood. I let her know that she was not alone, and most important, I shared with her how I got through it and made it through to the other side, a stronger person for it. I would like to say that it was all part of the plan, but I was really just shooting from the hip. I intuitively felt that it was the only way I could relate to the situation. As it turned out, what I told her took her by complete surprise, as well, and we had a very strong moment where we both knew that everything was going to be OK.

We talked about it several times after that, and I walked her through this same process that you are going through now, but at the time, we did it all verbally. Karen recovered from the experience quickly and was able to become stronger as a result. She is a brave individual who has grown to help others. We pushed each other to be better, and that's what this is all about: identifying the problem and supporting one another through it like family.

I didn't know it at the time, but this experience would become the foundation of Phase 4 and solidify my belief that sharing one's experience of getting truthful, opening up, and exposing the issues is a surefire way to true inner happiness. So let's look at the ways you can give back that will effectively help you to make this program a permanent part of your everyday life.

Giving Back

You will achieve no greater gain from the Turning Point than that which you get from helping others. Practicing Phase 4 in your everyday life ensures that you will never slip back into past thinking. Helping others and giving back what you have gained in this process will get you out of your own mind in the most productive way possible. It will set you on a course of productivity and a give you a profound sense of oneness with those around you. Now, it's just about putting one foot in front of the other and taking action.

If you've made it this far, you can certainly help someone else, so now it's just about finding those in need. Luckily, we at the Turning Point have thought about this phase extensively. The entire foundation of our brand is the simple idea of people helping people to get better at whatever they choose to take on.

It's imperative that we all work together and support one another on our journeys to our goals and beyond. That is the reason for our forum and the reason for this program of personal growth. Having completed the first three phases, you are armed with the tools to start helping others, so why not get started right away?

Turning Point Forum

The best place to start is right on the same forum where you likely shared the stories of your past and received assistance with your struggles. Now, it is time to return the favor. On the forum, you will find stories from others who are struggling with their problems. But before you start lending your virtual ear, let's go over some guidelines.

First and foremost, the Turning Point forum is strictly for support and truthful dialogue between fellow human beings. It is vitally important to remain positive in your approach and leave criticism behind. This is not an area for judgment; it's a safe haven for growth and sharing. Negativity and infighting will be quickly blocked from the group, ensuring an environment where people feel comfortable to share their experiences, growth, and goals.

So what is the proper way to help someone who opens up about a problem? That's the question you should be asking yourself. In my experience, the most effective way to talk to someone about a problem is to relate it to one of your own struggles. I will typically lead with something that happened to me and share how I got through it. I try to be as detailed as possible, explaining the way I felt at the time and how I feel about the issue today. It's extremely important that if you are trying to help someone, that the person knows that you have felt the same way and were able to get through it. There are several different possible approaches, so you will have to find out what works best for your personality, but you will always have to be able to relate the other person's story to your own in order to have your message heard and absorbed by others.

Never tell others what to do when it comes to their personal lives and actual life decisions. Rather, you should explain what you did when confronted with a similar situation or offer a few different suggestions based on your experience with the subject matter.

Help us to make the Turning Point forum a place where people can come after a tough day to support others and grow in a positive way!

Personal Friends

Offering support to personal friends is one of the easier ways that you can get started helping others. We all know people who have struggles. They are all around us, posting their problems on social media sites and endlessly complaining about how the deck is stacked against them.

But beware, you must not take a preachy approach with those who know you. People who know you well may take your attempts to help as a form of judgment. Often, approaching close friends with an offer of help takes more time than approaching those you don't know as well, and there's a simple reason for that: They need to see how you have changed before they will accept you as an authority.

Typically, when it comes to close friends, I wait until they notice how I have changed and decide to ask what's going on with me. Since I changed my personal story in such a dramatic way, friends who knew me before often ask how I managed to change so much. Change is, after all, quite difficult, as you surely know if you have worked through the phases correctly!

When someone asks me for help, I always take the same approach. I ask the person one simple question: "What are you willing to do to change your entire life?" This may seem dramatic, but that's exactly why I say it. If you are not willing to go to great lengths to change, than you will probably not change at all. It's pretty simple, really.

I typically do whatever I can to help those around me; however, one piece of advice I will share with you is that in certain cases, you should just keep your growth to yourself! You probably know the kind of friends I'm talking about. With people like that, just wait until they come to you.

Family

Believe it or not, helping family members is probably the most difficult challenge of all. I've found that people are much more likely to listen to complete strangers than to family members about issues concerning personal growth. It's primarily because of the long history we've had with our loved ones that makes broaching this topic so difficult. That doesn't mean it's impossible, but always exercise caution, so you don't shut yourself out from being able to help the people in your family down the road.

The primary reason I know this book is going to work for you is because you sought it out. You are ready and willing to change. That's not true for everyone, though, and it's quite important that you keep that in mind when dealing with family. I always recommend waiting until people are good and ready for change before diving in to help. I promise you, if you change first, people will want to know how — it's human nature. When we see others happy, we get curious; so be happy, and people will come to you.

The closer someone is to you, the more important it is to practice patience. Believe me, when you start bounding though goals that eluded you in the past, people will definitely stop and take notice. Be on the ready when they approach you to deliver your personal message of how they too can change, providing they are willing to do things a little differently.

Co-Workers

We spend the majority of our time around our co-workers; most likely you already have your eyes on some people who could use these phases in their life. When it comes to matters affecting your workplace, I highly recommend just passing along a suggestion of where you found this program. Work is how you pay your bills and provide for your family. It would be irresponsible for us at the Turning Point to suggest trying to promote a program such as this where you make your living.

True Growth Elsewhere

We've already discussed how you can help those close to you and those over on the Turning Point forum. There is one more life-changing experience that you can pursue that I highly recommend. Charity and service to your fellow man will turbo-boost your growth. Giving and expecting nothing in return will pay dividends that you never expected. I get more out of giving my time for a good cause than the effort I put into it every time. The best part about it is that it's free and only requires a little bit of your time.

Think about it this way: One hour is equivalent to 4 percent of your day or 0.6 percent of your week. People usually whip out their calculators when I reel off these numbers. Would you be willing to trade 0.6 percent of your week to feel amazing about yourself? I would, and I do. The payoff from helping others while expecting nothing in return is all internal, and it's the best type of self-help you can imagine — once you have worked through the four phases of the Turning Point program. Remember, without clearing the past, efforts such as charity and service to others are like aspirin for a migraine — they don't really help all that much. But once we get the issues of our past out of the way, charity and service become something totally different. They will give you a feeling of accomplishment that you can take home with you and feel good about without reverting back to the feelings of the past.

How do you get started with something like this? Thankfully, the Internet has made it incredibly easy, but in case you don't like searching too much, I recommend visiting www.volunteermatch.org.

Go into this process expecting nothing in return. Go into it with enthusiasm, and you will reap rewards you never thought possible.

Conclusion

Let's review where you've been on this journey. In Phase 1, you listed your prior goals and possible reasons for failing to achieve them. In Phase 2, you dug deep into your past to find your part in events that controlled you through guilt, fear, and doubt, as well as getting truthful about people you had hurt. In Phase 3, you made things right concerning your past behavior and circumstances, to the best of your abilities. Finally, in Phase 4, you gave away what you had learned about yourself, in a nonjudgmental way. Additionally, you learned that you must find the time to help others less fortunate than yourself to optimize your growth.

I find it hard to believe that anyone could possibly go through a process such as this without learning countless things about his or her capabilities and inner self. There is no magic pill to happiness, but there is a way out of the dark. It's only through shining the light deeply within yourself that you can root out the best you within.

I assure you that if you've made it to this point and followed through with each phase of the Turning Point process, you are well on your way to blowing through future goals and readdressing that part in Phase 1 where you spelled out your goals from the past. I applaud you for making it this far. My guess is that it hasn't been easy; perhaps you've put this book down and picked it up several times. Or perhaps you have just read straight through without actually trying to complete the process. You may think that it won't work for you. If so, check to see if the message is coming from the part of your mind that always tells you to give up.

Whatever your path is from here, I hope it lines up with the direction in which you want to go. Your personal growth is *your* responsibility, which makes it all the more painful if you fail. Having made it through this process, you have cemented in place a foundation on which you can build your future the way you always intended. Attack your goals with passion, drive, and enthusiasm. Never get discouraged. Stay positive in your approach, and you will

surely cross whatever finish line you have set
for yourself.

Turning Point: Meditation

Next Steps

At this point, you might well be thinking, "Now what?" You've worked through the four Turning Point phases and built a foundation from which to grow successfully, but what's the next step on your path to achieving personal growth and success, however you define it? Don't worry, there's a plan for that, too. In the upcoming chapters, I'll show you a variety of proven methods for keeping yourself on track and getting yourself where you want to go. The first two steps are focusing your mind and setting realistic, achievable goals. And that's what we're going to cover in the next couple of chapters: Meditation and Goal Construction.

Meditation: The Path to Peace

You're stressed, anxious, and always too busy. But stop and think: Have you ever been caught in a moment, stuck, staring at something — perhaps water in a stream flowing over rocks, a tree swaying in the wind, or clouds drifting across the sky? In that small moment, your mind is hyper-focused on one thing. Time seems to slow down. You aren't thinking about work or bills or your obligations. Imagine being able to tap into that moment for a more extended time, whenever you wish. Your mind is yearning for such moments, and with a little practice, you can reboot and reset your mind, clean the slate, and reconnect with a different perspective.

I've covered a lot of ground with the Turning Point program already. If you've taken the steps I've outlined along the way, you've been moving straight ahead through each phase of the program. Now, though, I'm going to ask you to move off that straight-line path and take a few steps sideways for a while, away from your usual way of thinking.

You see, I couldn't get the problems I struggled with in my life under control until I seriously attacked the steps and phases outlined earlier. Yet as I worked through each one, I began to suspect my mind was a lot more powerful than I realized. Meditation showed me how I could learn how to tap into those hidden capabilities. I want to tell you how meditation can help you use your mind to serve you in new and powerful ways.

At first, meditation may *seem* to be a step into strange territory. Eventually, though, you'll see that once you understand it and have practiced it for a little while, meditation no longer seems strange. After that, you'll realize it's the giant step you've looked for your entire life. Meditation puts you back on the straight-line path better equipped, happier, and more peaceful than you ever imagined you could be.

Meditation can magnify and strengthen the benefits you get from every other aspect of your life and from the Turning Point program. It's a tool that can bring real peace into your life. Peace — without the worries, fears, and concerns over what has already happened or what may yet occur.

In this brief introduction to meditation, we'll cover the following topics:

- What is meditation?
- How does meditation help people?
- Instructions for successful meditation
- Gaining new perspectives through meditation
- Understanding the difference between you and your thoughts

What Is Meditation?

"Yesterday is history, tomorrow is a mystery, and today is a gift; that's why they call it the present."

—Anonymous

Psychology Today defines meditation as "the practice of turning your attention to a single point of reference. It can involve focusing on the breath, on bodily sensations, or on a word or phrase known as a mantra. In other words, meditation means turning your attention away from distracting thoughts and focusing on the present moment."[1]

We humans have some rather bizarre habits, and ignoring the present moment is one of the strangest. Most people spend their time thinking of only two things: the past and the future. Stop reading for a moment, and consider that statement carefully. You habitually think of only two things: the past and the future.

When we think of the past, we might occasionally recall a happy time with friends, a vacation getaway, or some other memorable occasion. But too often, we remember wrongs we have committed, things that embarrassed us, things we regret, or things for which we blame ourselves. In other words, recalling the past often includes beating ourselves up for failures in word or deed.

Thinking about the future is nearly as pointless. Much of what we think about the future is based on experiences we've had in the past. A man may fear losing his job because he's had a spotty employment record. A woman may fear losing her partner because she's seen it happen to her friends. A person may worry about a home invasion or being beaten and robbed because it's happened elsewhere in the neighborhood. Thinking about the future often involves worry — fearing what might happen.

Instead of constantly thinking about the past and the future, you can choose to take time out to live in the present moment. That's what meditation allows you to do. However, you might well say, "The present only lasts an instant. Why should I think about it? I need to prepare for the future, and the past is my best guide."

That's a great objection and a great question. And here's the answer:

Your brain continually plays thoughts, like a radio that never turns off. In many ways, your brain isn't much different than any other organ in your body. Your stomach, for example, uses all kinds of biological and chemical processes to digest food. That's what it does. Your heart pumps blood; your lungs send oxygen to your body. Each of these organs has evolved through millions of years to do specific things. Your brain's job is to play thoughts into your awareness.

No doubt, you are proud of your brain. You probably think of it as the defining characteristic of who you are, and you don't want to think of it as just a thought-producing machine. But consider this: From an evolutionary standpoint, the thoughts our brains produce have served to keep us alive in a dangerous environment. When a cave man heard a rustling in the bushes, his brain warned him of a tiger stalking him. The human brain became our guide, showing us how to avoid life's dangers. But in these modern, civilized times, our brains still constantly bubble up thoughts based on "what if" scenarios. What if my boss fires me? How will I pay my bills? Or what if the person I love leaves me? What will I do then?

Such "what if" questions have become today's modern equivalent of the tiger in the bushes. Our brains serve up thoughts to solve problems that don't exist except as worries about the future.

Those thoughts alternate between the dead past and countless possible futures, always seeming to offer guidance on how to live life.

But there's something you really need to understand. *Your brain is not your mind.* Your mind is far more than the three-pound bundle of neurons squeezed into your head; it transcends the physical. Your mind can open new channels of understanding, wisdom, and knowledge when you let it. Living in the present through meditation gives you access to those new channels.

How Will Meditation Help?

In 1971, Harvard Medical School researcher Herbert Benson, M.D., coined the term "relaxation response" when studying the effect meditation had upon its practitioners. Since then, more than 3,000 scientific studies have shown that meditation helps improve people's quality of life in many ways. It's been shown to help with health and physical ailments, such as improved immune response, lower levels of inflammation, and decreased sensitivity to pain. It improves thinking, decision-making, and overall mental functioning. Brain-imaging studies show that meditation sharpens attention and memory. It also improves emotional well-being and has been linked to increased happiness and greater compassion.

From among these thousands of studies, there are a few findings that you might find especially relevant in your life. Meditation has been shown to result in:

- **Less anxiety and depression**. People who meditate report that they enjoy and appreciate life more than nonmeditators. They find that meditating helps improve their relationships.

- **Stability and equanimity.** Meditation brings about feelings of balance, often described as tranquility, composure, and calmness. According to Michael J. Baime, M.D., director of the Penn Program for Mindfulness, "Meditation cultivates an emotional stability that allows the meditator to experience intense emotions fully while simultaneously maintaining perspective on them."[2] Meditators can thus achieve greater insight and understanding about their thoughts, feelings, and actions.
- **Clarity of mind.** Do you sometimes find yourself flip-flopping when trying to make a decision, wondering which choice is the best and feeling confused and uncertain? Meditation can transform your mind to one that's calm and clear, without agitation. Meditation clears away confusion and helps you make better decisions.

- **Reduce alcohol and substance abuse.** Clinical studies suggest that meditation can lead to a reduction in alcohol and substance abuse.
- **Reduce the effects of panic and anxiety attacks.** Mindfulness meditation can lessen the symptoms of anxiety and panic. Additionally, the practice of meditation can help maintain those beneficial outcomes in people with generalized anxiety disorder, panic disorder, or panic disorder with agoraphobia.

If you'd like to read the scientific studies behind these findings yourself, visit the Resources section of this chapter for references that discuss the many benefits and positive outcomes you can expect from meditation.

How to Meditate

Just as physical exercise trains the body, meditation trains the mind. If you go to the gym and hire a personal trainer, you'll find that each trainer has different preferred methods and techniques. Likewise, there are many forms and styles of meditation. You may have heard of transcendental meditation, mindfulness meditation, Vipassana, Zen, mantra meditation and many other types with roots in Buddhism and Hinduism. With so many choices, you could well ask where to begin.

First, it's important to understand that these many forms exist because each of them works. There is no "best" form of meditation.

Second, it's equally important to understand what meditation is not. It is not reaching some kind of trancelike state. It's not a matter of getting "blissed out." It's not about "emptying your mind" and finding nirvana. It's not something you do to get high or to achieve some kind of mystical altered state.

What all styles of meditation have in common is that they focus attention. You can think of "attention" as a special kind of thought —a thought that watches other thoughts. So meditation is a matter of thinking about thinking.

Step 1: *Finding Your Attention*

Try this right now:

1.Sit comfortably and relax. Uncross your arms and legs. Let your feet rest on the floor. Close your eyes. Take a couple of deep breaths. Let your shoulders relax and fall.

2.Notice that your thoughts might take the form of words, phrases or sentences. Or they may paint a picture in your mind's eye. Sit quietly for a few minutes and notice which form your thoughts take at each moment. Notice how they may change.

3.Each time you notice a new thought, say out loud either "words" or "images." Or, if you don't want to speak, you can raise one thumb or the other to acknowledge either words or images.

When you do this, you're discovering your ability to watch your thoughts. You're training your attention. You're noticing how your thoughts continuously surface without conscious control, just like that radio that never stops playing. Most important, you're discovering that there is something about thinking that's beyond simply responding to whatever your brain puts out while it runs on autopilot. Namely, you have found your attention. You now know you can *focus your attention on your thinking.* That's the first step in learning to meditate.

I suggest you practice this for a few minutes at a time, four or five times today. Tomorrow, practice again until you can quickly find your attention and begin tabulating the kind of thoughts you are having. As you practice focusing your attention, you'll notice that your everyday thoughts don't just bubble up constantly — they cover an incredible range of topics. That turbulence you'll find in your thinking has sometimes been called the "monkey mind" because it jumps from one topic to another so often. You could even say we humans are addicted to thinking. We can't control it, and we certainly can't stop it. We seem to need that constant "fix," whether it's a thought about the past or the future. So let's move to the second step in learning to meditate.

Step 2: *Becoming Mindful*

Mindfulness meditation is the most widely taught form of meditation in the United States. It asks you to intentionally focus on the present moment. It asks you to accept and pay attention to the thoughts, sensations, and emotions that arise without judging them. We'll use your breath as a tool to help you learn to meditate. Simply do this:

1.Sit comfortably and relax. Uncross your arms and legs. Let your feet rest on the floor. Close your eyes. Take a few of deep breaths. Let your shoulders relax and fall.

2.Focus your attention on your breathing as you inhale and exhale. You might notice your breath moving through your nostrils. Or you might notice your breath as your chest balloons out with each inhale and then falls with each exhale. It doesn't matter what physical sensation you use to notice your breathing. Your goal is to direct your attention to the constant inflow and outflow of breath.

3.When you inhale, be aware that you're breathing in and focus on how it feels. When you exhale, be aware of the exhale and how it feels. Keep your focus in the moment-by-moment sensation of your breathing.

4.As you become mindful of your breath, you'll notice thoughts bubbling up and drawing your attention away from your breath. You'll get distracted by external sounds, sensations, mind's-eye imagery, and random thoughts. Each time that happens, simply notice the distraction and recognize the fact that you've been distracted for an instant. Allow the distraction to go where it will as you return your attention to your breath. You'll find there is no need to judge the distraction. Don't condemn it or wish it away. Simply notice it happening; then, return your attention to your breathing.

5.Continue this accepting, nonjudgmental process for five to 10 minutes. You don't need to add anything to each moment-by-moment experience or sensation. Just be aware of what happens as it happens, without getting carried away by any thoughts that cross your mind. As you practice this form of meditation, you can gradually extend the time you spend in meditation, with the goal of eventually spending 30 minutes in each daily session.

A distraction could be an external sound, an itch, the need to cough or yawn, a draft of cold air, or someone entering the room. No matter what distracts you from focusing on your breathing, the distraction is always a thought. All of those stimuli become thoughts before you can recognize them.

Mindfulness meditation shows you how to observe all those random and wandering thoughts as they drift through your mind. Your goal is to avoid getting involved or carried away with them and to avoid judging them. Instead, you want to cultivate a simple awareness of each thought as it arises.

With practice, you'll begin seeing how your thoughts and feelings tend to move in certain patterns. Gradually, you'll become more aware of your natural tendency to quickly judge thoughts as happy or sad, good or bad, welcome or worrisome, pleasant or unpleasant. You'll begin realizing how you've learned to categorize, pigeonhole, and judge almost every thought that runs through your mind. With practice, you'll find that an inner balance develops that allows you to simply *be* with whatever happens — in the moment and without judgment.

Reimagining the World

Once you begin practicing meditation, you'll start making some amazing discoveries. You'll begin forming a new view of your life and the world around you. Here's a preview of two of the most important new perspectives you'll gain.

Taming Dukkha

Dukkha is a term used in Buddhism that is often translated as "anxiety," "stress," "suffering," or "unsatisfactoriness." The word comes from the Sanskrit and means "a wheel out of kilter."

Imagine riding in a car with one wheel that wasn't quite round. On every revolution, you feel the car bump or bounce. No matter what you do, there's no cure for the rough ride. Driving at low speeds is tolerable, at least for a short trip, but as you accelerate or take longer trips, the bounce becomes truly annoying — maybe even intolerable. It will begin to feel like the car is going to self-destruct. The Buddha applied this metaphor to our lives — although he probably used an ox cart instead of a car! *Dukkha* is knowing deep down that something basic and important about life is not quite right. While life may bring you pleasure, the annoyance always returns because your life is fundamentally flawed. This persistent anxiety, suffering, and stress manifests itself in at least two ways.

The first is through pain. Physical and emotional pain are both unavoidable parts of human life. You might be able to dampen these feelings or to medicate against them. But you can't avoid pain over the long haul, and this is a major source of stress, suffering, and anxiety — *dukkha*. Trying to avoid pain is a natural human tendency, but in the end, everyone needs to face up to it. After all, we'll all die eventually, whether through sickness or some traumatic event that kills us.

Meditation improves your ability to minimize pain by "going into" the pain itself. The average person might stub a toe and start cursing, shouting, and hopping around on one foot. He might curse himself, the piece of furniture he walked into, or the gods above. A seasoned meditator will simply acknowledge the pain rather than shouting out a story about it. Studies have shown over and over that "being with" pain dramatically reduces its impact.

Change is another unavoidable aspect of human life, and it's another cause of *dukkha*. No matter what we think, what we talk about, or what we care about, everything around us is in a constant state of flux. The weather changes each moment, as does the stock market. So does our affection, compassion, and caring for one another. A married couple may find their love has turned to hate, so they divorce. There is literally *nothing* that doesn't change. Therein lies a real problem, because most of us want to preserve the *status quo.* We want to pin down reality so that it meets our wants and needs. We take nearly insane steps to keep things as they are while everything in the universe moves toward change. We try to control what is happening now and what will happen next. That's a profound challenge and one that is guaranteed to be a losing battle. It's the cause of endless misery for people who can't "go with the flow."

Our Milky Way galaxy, along with tens of thousands of other galaxies, is flying at a breakneck speed of 14 million miles per hour toward a mysterious, unknown force cosmologists have dubbed the Great Attractor. In the face of such incomprehensible events happening all on their own without the slightest input from any of us, what amount of arrogance, vanity, and self-importance could we possibly have to believe we can control what is? Meditation shows you how living in the present moment eliminates the seemingly natural but disastrous human drive to control people, events, and situations.

Meditation Heals Harmful Habits

We all have habits that don't serve us well. Among these are:

- The tendency to be judgmental.
- Placing expectations on people, situations, and events.
- An eagerness to make demands on others.

Judgments, expectations, and demands are an unholy trinity of habits that most humans carry around without even noticing. Let's break them down.

Judgments

When you judge another person, a situation, or an event, you invariably do so from your own personal perspective. Even though your perspective may be shared by millions of others, it's equally likely that there are millions more with different points of view. Judging can be risky business, because it tends to make people feel separate from one another rather than connected.

Imagine you're sitting in a conference room filled with people. As you look around, you notice someone sitting a few tables away and instantly judge that person as being unlikable. Perhaps you make that judgment because of the way he is dressed or based on his race or ethnicity. Maybe it's because of his body language, his boisterous voice, or his facial expression. Shortly, the moderator calls the meeting to order and introduces that person as the guest speaker. As he stands behind the podium, he engages the entire audience, including you. Now, you like him.

We judge most everything and everyone we encounter. Meditation can gradually show you the futility of trying to impose your judgment on the world around you. You'll eventually find the answer to the question, "Who am I to judge?" As you continue your meditation practice, you may well find it possible to leave judgment behind.

Expectations

It's reasonable to expect the sun to rise tomorrow or for your loved ones to care about your welfare. But it's damaging to place expectations on people, events, and situations. Some years ago, I bought an airline ticket to visit a relative I hadn't seen in a long time. When I arrived at the airport, I called her. She said she was tired and asked if I could come to see her the next day. I had been looking forward to the reunion. Not wanting to see me until the next day could have been disappointing; it could have led me to complain or accuse her of being rude. Neither of those reactions would have endeared us to one another. So I dropped my expectation, found something to do, and reconnected with her the next day. We both had a great time.

Meditation can help you suspend your expectations rather than burdening the other person (and yourself) with negative emotions when things don't work out the way you expect. It helps you see that events simply unfold as the world marches on; there's seldom any reason to let that unfolding upset you.

Demands

People in relationships — whether they're family, friends, work associates, or connected in some other way — tend to put demands on one another. Spouses expect their partners to play certain roles and do certain things. People in work environments have bosses who make demands of them. However, putting undue demands on other people can lead to conflict and emotional upset.

Consider the man who expects his wife to take care of the "women's work" around the house. Many women would feel that his demand to play a worn-out, last-century role is unwelcome. Likewise, the boss who expects his administrative assistant to take care of his dry cleaning is stepping over the line. Placing demands on others needs to be done with care and consideration. Meditation can help you see the oneness of all humanity, leading to a greater respect for each person in any kind of relationship.

The Final Lesson

As you learn meditation, you'll recognize that *the thoughts produced by your brain are not who you are.* Your thoughts are turbulent and constantly changing because you're filled with desires, wants, needs, and frustrations. You want too many things. It might seem as if there's never enough money, time, fun, or love to fulfill you. You live with a constant sense of lack, and the *dukkha* I explained earlier guarantees that life remains difficult.

At the same time, you fear too many things to be comfortable, so you try to avoid situations that make those fearful events come true. Meditation can help you overcome both your attraction to the things you want and your aversion to those you fear. It does that by validating — in terms you cannot ignore — that *you are not your thoughts!* What you think does not define what or who you are.

You are more than a body controlled by a brain. You are a spiritual essence housed in a body, and you are unique and special. Through meditation, you may come to regard the spiritual aspect of what you are as the most important part.

If you take your journey into meditation seriously, you may eventually come to a more advanced form of meditation. It isn't something you need to strive for. In fact, striving and meditating are incompatible. However, you may reach a level of meditation where you can successfully stop thinking for rather extended periods of time. When you meditate with a wholly empty mind, your attention moves beyond the ordinary world into finer realms that can give you access to great wisdom and open your intuitive nature.

For the most advanced meditators — Zen masters and the like — the deepest level of meditation is one without thought of any kind. For those, the mind becomes tranquil — at peace with the universe and all that is. The perception of time flowing like a river is replaced with the certain knowledge that eternity simply *is;* that the past and the future are nothing more than illusory constructs.

Conclusion

People have practiced meditation for more than 7,000 years, and dozens of cultures have refined meditative techniques through the centuries. Today, with modern equipment such as functional MRI brain scanning, we know more about meditation and its effects than any generation in history. Yet meditation straddles science and spirituality. It brings two disparate belief systems together and forces modern science to consider what the ancients took on faith. Meditation transcends the physical, yet it exerts dramatic effects upon the brain and virtually every bodily system.

Meditation is a practice that can become a lifelong habit. This chapter only brushes the surface. However, if you follow the simple instructions offered earlier, you'll discover a world of new thought. The biggest hurdle you'll face in learning to meditate is setting aside time for practice every day. If blocking out 30 minutes daily is too difficult, start with 15 minutes daily. Over time, you may find you can gradually move toward the 30-minute target. On the other hand, if time is not a problem, you might choose to work toward an hour daily.

Learning any new skill takes time and a good deal of dedication and effort. But with practice, meditation gives you a new way of relating to your thoughts and emotions. It lets you choose how you think and, by extension, enables you to become who you genuinely are.

There are additional resources on meditation available on the Turning Point website, including a complete eight-week online course that teaches mindfulness meditation in depth. The program, created by Dr. Jon Kabat-Zin, founder of the mindfulness method, is the same program offered at the University of Massachusetts and elsewhere.

Be sure to check out all the resources, and make meditation a part of your life.

References and Resources

For detailed instruction, help, and information regarding meditation, visit these websites:

- Live and Dare (www.liveanddare.com): An excellent resource for people seeking to learn meditation.
- Palouse Mindfulness (palousemindfulness.com): A free, online, eight-week self-guided training program in mindfulness meditation.
- Practicing Mindfulness: An Introduction to Meditation (www.thegreatcourses.com/courses/practicing-mindfulness-an-introduction-to-meditation.html): A 24-lesson course on mindfulness meditation presented by Professor Mark Muesse; available to stream, on CD, or on DVD.

[1] Meditation, Psychology Today, **https://www.psychologytoday.com/basics/meditation**

[2] Meditation, The Free Dictionary, **http://medical-dictionary.thefreedictionary.com/meditation**

Turning Point: Goal Construction

Setting goals may seem like the easiest thing in the world, but creating goals that you will actually achieve is a much more daunting challenge. Despite the abundance of New Year's resolutions made each year, only a small fraction — perhaps as few as 8 percent — are actually successful. That means 9 out of 10 people fail to achieve their big, shiny new goals each year.

I used to be one of those people. When I was struggling in my life, I would set goal after goal, only to see them crumble before me. This repeated failure to actually make progress toward the things I wanted left me feeling stuck, frustrated, and more alone than ever.

So what sets those who succeed in achieving their goals apart from those who fail?

There is no special personality type that makes a person more likely to successfully reach a goal. I struggled my whole life to stick to the resolutions I set, but then I learned a better way to set and reach my goals. Mastering a few simple strategies can transform the way you look at goals and will set in motion the change you need to alter your entire life.

Crafting Goals That Put You on a Path to Success

Clarifying Your Life Values

"When your values are clear to you, making decisions becomes easier."
— widely attributed to Roy E. Disney

One of the most essential steps in creating effective goals actually has very little to do with your goals themselves. Instead, it involves values.

Values are at the root of how we run our lives. What are your values? They include how you view the world, the things you consider important, and what you believe. Values and goals are different. Values are ideals. You can never "achieve" a value, although you can certainly alter your life to be more consistent with your values.

In contrast, a goal represents a specific and attainable objective. A goal may or may not be in line with your overall life values.

Before I worked through the Turning Point phases in my own life, every goal I set ended in failure. For me, the transformation occurred when I realized that those goals were not truly aligned with my values. You are much more likely to succeed at a goal if it is motivated by your core, inner values. That's why it is so important to stop and really think about your values before you set a single goal.

Faith and fear both demand you believe in something you cannot see.

You choose.

Identifying your values may feel challenging or confusing. By their very nature, values are intangible. We don't talk a lot about them in day-to-day life. In fact, this whole discussion of values may seem completely foreign to you! Regardless, your values form the very core of who you are and who you want to become. This makes your values an extraordinarily powerful force that can shift you onto an entirely different life path.

Values Exercise

It's important to note that everything in the Turning Point is a program of action. As with most things in life, you are going to get out as much as you put in. Because everyone is different, each of us is motivated by different things. This means that there are no one-size-fits-all solutions. It is imperative to be absolutely fearless and search down deep when looking at yourself and your path to change. There are times when you will find out new things about yourself that you never knew before. By putting in a little work, you will create your own path and expand your life in ways you never expected.

Begin by sitting down with a pen and a piece of paper. Write down all of the things you value, no matter whether they feel right or wrong to you. Critiquing or second-guessing your values at this stage doesn't help. Here are some questions to get your thinking started:

- Imagine that you have a day entirely to yourself. Where would you go, and what would you do? Would you be alone or with someone else? Money, everyday errands, and time constraints are no object. Then, think about why you would choose those activities for your perfect day. Did your day sound comforting? Adventurous? Quietly contented? Bold or dramatic?

- Think back over the past few years of your life. Consider moments when you have felt excited or motivated. Even if those moments seem few and far between, we all have scraps of time that energize or excite us. What were you doing in those moments? If you can't think of specific examples, then make a list of new things that you think would motivate or energize you.

- Consider your belief system. What contributes to your sense of right and wrong? If you believe in a higher power, think about the role your religion or spirituality plays in your life. For nonbelievers, what anchors your moral compass? As you consider the factors that motivate your sense of rightness, it will become easier to discern your life values.

- Think about the phrase "a life worth living." What does that life look like to you? If you had that life, which facets of your current life would be the same as they are now, and which would be different?
- What makes you feel most peaceful and contented? Where are you when you feel this way? Who is with you? What have you been doing?

When answering these questions, keep in mind that your values may feel intangible and your aspirations unattainable. At this point in your goal-setting journey, that is perfectly fine. Our values hint at what we desire in the deepest, most secret places in our hearts. If you're having trouble articulating your values, consider some of the following things that people often value:

- Achievement
- Activeness
- Adventure
- Beauty/attractiveness
- Bravery
- Calmness
- Charity/generosity
- Community involvement
- Contentedness
- Creativity
- Devotion
- Efficiency
- Empathy
- Environmental-mindedness
- Fame
- Family
- Financial security
- Fitness
- Friendships
- Harmony
- Health

- Humor/fun
- Integrity
- Intellectualism
- Job security
- Leadership
- Liberty
- Originality
- Power
- Religion/spirituality
- Resourcefulness
- Risk-taking
- Self-discipline
- Sexuality
- Trust
- Truthfulness
- Wealth
- Wisdom

Keep in mind that there are no "good" or "bad" values. I often see people getting caught up in evaluating their own values. They allow their fears or self-doubt to make them critical about the things that matter to them. For example, people sometimes ask me whether valuing financial security, attractiveness, or fame makes them shallow. However, digging deeper into these values often shows that they are about a desire for connection to others, valuing oneself as a person, or seeking stability. Those aren't shallow desires at all. In fact, these values are natural manifestations of things we've all experienced at one time or another. Accepting your values without judgment is the first step in transforming your life to be in line with what matters most to you.

Connecting Values to Goals

Now that you have brainstormed your list of values, it is time to learn how to connect those with your goals. Goals are specific, attainable objectives. They may or may not be in line with the things you value.

For example, perhaps your list of values includes connections with others, contentedness, empathy, and health. Let's look at some goals that are connected to those values versus some goals that are not.

One possible goal might be "to get back together with my ex." On its surface, this seems like a perfectly reasonable goal. After all, a person who values connections with others may seek to repair a connection that was lost. And rekindling a damaged relationship is often a good way to practice empathy toward others. However, it's important to dig a little deeper into the motivation for this goal. Why do you want to achieve it? What value does it really fulfill? Are you simply trying to avoid feeling alone? Perhaps you want to feel good about yourself by apologizing for past wrongs. Do you really believe that you will achieve an honest, supportive relationship with this person?

After some reflection, you might recall that your relationship with your ex was a bit tumultuous. You were constantly arguing and were never on the same page about anything. That doesn't sound like a very contented life, does it? You may also remember that your ex liked to go out to bars a lot, so you drank quite a bit more heavily when you were together. This doesn't exactly align with your value of health. After looking at your values and your goals, it may become clear that although rekindling a relationship with your ex would provide you with a connection to someone else, the relationship wouldn't actually get you any closer to living in line with your values.

Now, let's consider how you could craft a goal that *is* in line with your values. Because you value connections with others, this goal will be about your relationships with other people. This might mean a romantic relationship or it could mean strengthening a friendship or a relationship with a family member. You also value contentedness, which means that you're looking for a person who will provide stability and support.

Perhaps a good goal would be "to meet new people or improve relationships with people in my life who provide emotional support for me." This also aligns with your value of health, as emotionally supportive people are often those who help keep us on a track to healthy living. To get more specific, you might think about joining a yoga class to meet new people or calling your brother at least once a week. These are tangible ways to achieve your goal of developing emotionally supportive relationships.

Let's consider another example; this one illustrates a classic trap. You are a sales representative for a pharmaceutical company. Your goal list includes family, community engagement, physical fitness, and financial security. Your company just advertised a new position that would be a promotion for you and comes with a bump in salary. It would also expand your sales territory, giving you additional potential to generate more income.

Your goal is to get this promotion and increase your earning power.

On its surface, this goal seems perfectly aligned with your value of financial security. By providing you with a greater income, the promotion will also mean that you can provide more things for your family. You plan to enroll your child in hockey lessons and buy an SUV that will make your family road trips more pleasant.

But here's what actually happens once you get the promotion: You work longer hours. Your expanded sales territory means you have to travel extensively and stay in hotels three or four nights a week. You also feel the need to work more on the weekends, cutting into what was previously family time. Additionally, because you feel so exhausted from your work schedule, you're not able to get up and go to the gym in the morning like you used to. You're also eating fewer healthy, home-cooked meals because you're on the road so often. As a result, you gain 10 pounds and feel constantly exhausted. You don't even have time to volunteer at your church or socialize with your friends anymore.

After fully assessing the situation, you may begin to question whether the goal of obtaining this job promotion truly aligns with your values. Sure, it will increase your income, helping you work toward your value of financial security. At the same time, though, it is setting you up for an exhausting lifestyle. This exhaustion makes it much less likely that you will feel involved with your family or engaged with your community. Being on the road so much also makes it challenging to stay physically fit, which is important to you.

When reflecting on your values, you might decide to set a different goal for yourself instead: "Find a way to create a flex-time schedule at work that maintains my income while giving me more time to be with my family." This will help you work toward financial security while giving you the flexibility to prioritize family time, community, and health. The more closely a goal aligns with your values, the more likely you will be to work hard to achieve it.

Do you see how easy it is to fall into the trap of setting goals that are directly contrary to your values? Things that seem like good opportunities — a promotion, a career change, rekindling a lost relationship, moving across the country — may actually keep you stuck in misery. After all, when our everyday lives do not align with our values, we feel off-kilter. This may lead to feelings of sadness, fear, anxiety, or depression.

Worst of all, failing to acknowledge your values prevents you from setting effective goals that will help you create the life you want.

Setting Appropriate Goals

"Setting goals is the first step in turning the invisible into the visible." — Tony Robbins

When you're eager to make changes in your life, it's easy to quickly jot down a few goals and try to get to work. Before I got my life together through the Turning Point phases, I was constantly setting new goals only to find myself failing at them every time. One of the reasons for this is that goal-setting takes work, and it takes a good strategy. Taking the time to carefully craft thoughtful, attainable goals will pay enormous dividends, because you'll be able to maintain momentum as you knock each one off your list.

There are no good or bad values, but there are good and bad goals. Appropriate goal-setting is a skill that takes some practice to master. Consider this example of a bad goal: "My New Year's resolution is to finally get

the body I want by losing 100 pounds."
While losing weight is an admirable
aspiration, this resolution makes a pretty
rotten goal. Not only is it unrealistic, but it's
not very specific. It doesn't answer the
question of how you're going to get to the
finish line or in what time frame.

Now, consider a better alternative: "I will
lose 10 pounds by March 1, with another 1
pound per week thereafter until I achieve a
total weight loss of 25 pounds." Look at the
aspects of this goal that make it different
from the 100-pound weight loss resolution.
This goal is achievable. Losing 1 pound per
week is a very sensible and medically
appropriate weight loss goal. Furthermore,
this goal sets time boundaries to help keep
you on track. You might not always meet the
precise time frames set in the goal, but the
goal's parameters provide a way to hold
yourself accountable along the way to your
overall weight loss objective.

Psychologists have spent decades discovering what makes some goals better than others. I applied many of these principles to my own life when I was working through the Turning Point phases. By crafting good goals, I was able to lose weight, improve my relationships, and become successful in business.

The key to my success was crafting goals that were on POINT. POINT is a handy acronym that will keep you on track as you develop your own goals. A goal that is on POINT is:

- **Precise.** Goals should be as precise as possible. The vague sentiment, "I want to get along with people better" will get you nowhere. A more precise goal is, "I will practice empathy toward my family members as a way of improving my relationships with them. This will include calling every week, listening to their concerns, and reflecting what they say back to them."

When making your goal precise, make sure it answers the questions "What?" "Why?" and "How?" This means it must include a plan for how you will measure your outcomes. Setting a precise goal is impossible if you do not have a way of measuring your progress. Perhaps your goal is to be more successful in your career. Unfortunately, "career success" is a very intangible and vague phrase. In fact, it could be considered more of a value. Some precise, measurable goals in this area might be: "Increase my income stream by $5,000 per year" or "Negotiate for a 7 percent raise within the next year" or "Expand my project management role by volunteering to manage three new projects next quarter." By simply looking at these goals, you can determine whether you have made progress toward them or not. They have distinct, easy-to-measure success metrics.

- **Obtainable.** The best goals are obtainable. Of course, given that you are setting the goal in the first place, it cannot be something you have already completed. However, it should be in line with your skills, knowledge, and capabilities. When determining if a goal is obtainable, ask yourself the following questions:
  - How will I complete this goal?
  - Do I have the resources I need to be successful, or can I work with someone else to develop those resources?
  - Do I feel challenged by this goal or simply overwhelmed?

Without the raw resources and capabilities to achieve your goals, you will quickly get stuck. This does not mean that you cannot be ambitious in your goal-setting. In fact, you should be! But it does mean that you need to keep your goals within the realm of the doable.

- **In line with values.** Goals that do not connect to your values are worthless. Take, for example, the goal of becoming a millionaire. We've all fantasized about having a lot of disposable money at some point or another. However, that money is worthless unless you do something with it. Without being connected to your values, your goals are just as purposeless. Dig deep to think of ways to live your life most fully with the values you've outlined, and let your goals flow from there.

- **Nourishing.** Setting goals is a way to prioritize yourself and your well-being. A good goal is nourishing for your body, mind, or spirit. Take the time to think of things that give you energy and provide a purpose for your time here on Earth. These might include family, friends, personal creativity, volunteer work, or aspects of your career. Setting goals that nourish you will not only add to your own well-being but will also help you find your place in the world.

- **Time-limited.** The best goals are time-limited. This means that there is a specific time frame built into each goal. Not only does this give you motivation to succeed, it also holds you accountable. Consider the goal "to become a regional sales manager." That is a perfectly admirable goal. Unfortunately, it does not provide a time frame for accomplishing the objective. Would you be happy if it took you 20 years to achieve that goal, and you got the position just a few months before you were ready to retire? It is important not to be *too* ambitious. For example, "Develop a stronger and more supportive relationship with my mother" is a goal that simply will not happen in a two-week timeframe. On the other hand, "Send my mother a card for her birthday, which is coming up in two weeks" is entirely achievable within that time period. The best time-limited goals create a sense of urgency without causing you to panic about how you will achieve them on time.

Dream Big and Set Value-Driven Goals

Now, take some time to generate a list of goals that you want to achieve. Remember to make them goals that are on POINT. Spend as much time as it takes to create goals that feel authentic and important to you. The goal-setting process is crucial to actually succeeding at your goals, so don't cut your time short during this critical planning stage.

I often get asked, "What is the magic number of goals I should shoot for?" The answer is that there is no magic number. Some people feel extraordinarily motivated by setting just one or two goals. Other people generate a list of 15 to 20 goals that they want to work on.

The key is to return to the guiding principle of Phase 1: honesty.

In Phase 1, you made a brutally honest assessment of your past and your present. You considered all of the goals you had previously set for yourself as well as why they never came to fruition. From childhood dreams to deadlines to milestones, you wrote everything down. Then, you examined the factors that led to these goals being uncompleted. This process of getting honest with yourself leaves many people feeling exhausted or even overwhelmed with their failures. However, it is the first step in creating a more authentic and transformative life.

You are now going to take the principle of getting honest and apply it to the goals you're setting for the future. Now that you know how to set good goals, there's a whole new world of possibilities! Leave no dream or ambition behind, no matter how fanciful or far-fetched it may seem. Even though we just discussed the importance of making your goals realistic and achievable, none of that matters in the early brainstorming stage. What is most important is that you tap into your inner, most authentic self. We will nurture the little wisps of hopes and dreams that you may have left for dead.

Exercise

Let's begin with a little exercise. Grab a pencil and some paper. Now, pretend that you are guaranteed to succeed, no matter what. Your fairy godmother has descended to help you out and promises that nothing will stand in your path. Take some time and write down all of the goals you would like to achieve. Do not let your fears, anxieties, or concerns about feasibility inhibit you. Simply let your mind and heart free to dream big dreams. This is the time for the goals you never thought were possible — to travel the world, to overcome your fear of public speaking, to leave an unhappy marriage, or to complete an Ironman triathlon.

Next, look at each goal and think, "How can I achieve this?" If you're anything like I used to be, you will immediately think, "There's no way I can achieve this. I'm not nearly smart or talented or strong enough for that." But don't let yourself get stuck in negative self-talk. If you are having trouble stepping out of that negative mindset, think of someone who you truly admire. Ask yourself what that person would do if faced with the prospect of figuring out how to achieve your goal. Think of any possible ways that you can take concrete steps toward achieving that goal.

Let's walk through an example together. Imagine that you are a customer service representative for a large cable company. You hate your job and feel completely unfulfilled by your work. However, it's a steady paycheck that keeps the rent paid.

When you were a teenager, you dreamed of becoming a best-selling author. You even had a short story published in your high school's literary magazine. However, after dropping out of college and starting a family, you decided it was too late to pursue your ambition. "After all," you thought, "there are probably thousands of wannabe authors out in the world who are trying to make it big. What's so special about me, anyway?"

OK, take a deep breath and set aside all of the negative judgments about yourself and your abilities. Your fantasy is to become a best-selling author. Ask yourself, "How can I achieve this goal?" Write down every possible way that you think you could make this happen, no matter how unlikely you think it might be. For example:

1.Go back to school to get my bachelor's degree in English followed by an M.F.A. or Ph.D. in creative writing.

2.Quit my job and devote myself full-time to writing a book.

3.Begin writing a novel during the hour I have each morning after the kids go to school and before I leave for work.

4.Pay an independent company to self-publish my work.

5.Meet the head of a large publishing house at a cocktail party and convince him or her to publish my book.

All of these are possible ways of achieving the goal of becoming a best-selling author. Notice how the list includes all kinds of possibilities, without any negative thinking or quibbles about what's realistic. Now, it's time to weigh each option. It's easy to set aside No. 2, as you currently depend on your income to pay the bills. However, as your writing career progresses, it is certainly a possibility that should remain on the table. You may also dismiss No. 5, which seems unlikely unless you have friends in the publishing business. Given your financial constraints, No. 1 and No. 4 may not seem particularly attractive at this time, although going back to school could certainly help you hone your craft.

However, when you take a closer look at No. 3, it doesn't seem so implausible. You have a quiet hour each morning that you currently spend unwinding and getting ready for a day at the job you hate. It wouldn't be so difficult to turn that into more productive writing time. In fact, you actually have another hour in the evening when you usually just watch TV. That makes two hours per day that you could devote to your budding writing career.

At this point, you have a potential path that could lead you toward achieving your goal of becoming a best-selling author. Of course, you cannot determine the publishing climate or the whims of book reviewers. However, you can set a few goals that are on POINT based on this plan. They might include:

1.I will write at least 500 words per day, five days per week, using my time in the morning after the kids go to school.

2.I will complete a draft of a 300-page novel within one year of today.

3.Within three months, I will become a participant in a fiction writing group in my community.

Within a few minutes, your wild fantasy of becoming a best-selling author just became a much more realistic possibility. Of course, it's unlikely that you will achieve your ultimate goal of writing a New York Times best-seller within the next year. However, with your current on-POINT goals, you will have a complete draft of a novel as well as feedback from other writers in your community. This places you much closer to your eventual goal of becoming a published author. It also fulfills your value of creativity, which has been stifled by your current job. Connecting your on-POINT goals back to your values will help your life feel more positive and balanced.

Be aware that if you set a large number of goals for yourself, you will not achieve them all right away. That's OK. It took years of your life to get to where you are today. Changing those bad habits and negative patterns takes hard work, perseverance, and a willingness to be radically honest with yourself.

Now, take some time to turn your wild, aspirational dreams into achievable goals that are on POINT. While it's important to dream big, breaking large goals down into more attainable chunks will help you maintain the motivation you need to succeed.

Getting Motivated to Achieve Your Goals: Addressing Your Fears

"If you set goals and go after them with all the determination you can muster, your gifts will take you places that will amaze you." — Les Brown

After completing a values assessment and writing your on-POINT goals, it's time to get motivated to succeed. Your goals will directly tie in to areas where you personally need to grow, right past wrongs that you have perpetrated, or put yourself on a new path. When I was at this point, I saw some pretty big changes I needed to make in my life. However, there was something still holding me back: fear.

We all have some fears. That's part of being human. Recognizing how those fears govern your life is essential for getting motivated to achieve your goals. Think about past goals you have set and why they failed. Something was keeping you stuck in your old patterns. What was it? When I ask people this question, they often point to another as the culprit: "My mom never thought I should go to college full-time, which is why I dropped out" or "My old boyfriend triggered a lot of body issues in me, which is why I don't date much anymore."

Dealing with your fears head-on is the best way to cultivate your motivation. Look closely at the fears and anxieties that are holding you back from attaining your goals. Have you, like many others, cultivated an identity around being a screw-up or a failure? If so, succeeding may feel like something that happens to other people, not you.

In many instances, it is the simple fear of failing that keeps people stuck. This is a tricky fear to deal with. In my case, it was helpful when I realized that many of my biggest idols had failed to achieve their goals — sometimes spectacularly. Michael Jordan didn't make his high school basketball team. J.K. Rowling's first Harry Potter novel was rejected by 12 different publishers. Thomas

Edison's teachers kicked him out of school, saying he was too stupid to learn. He is later reported to have said, "I have not failed. I've just found 10,000 ways that won't work."

What all of these people have in common is that they failed and kept on trying. All of us, even the ones who seem most successful, have failures in our past. And most of us have many failures awaiting us in the future. The critical point is that successful people keep trying despite the failures. They keep practicing free throws, continue to send out novel drafts to publishers, or persist in tinkering on electrical projects. Successful people use failures as learning opportunities, giving them the motivation to achieve their ambitious goals.

To get motivated, envision yourself achieving your goal. Let the feelings of triumph wash over you. Picture where you will be and who else will be there celebrating your success. Now, use that positive energy to propel yourself into action planning.

From Goal-Setting to Action Planning

"Our goals can only be reached through a vehicle of a plan, in which we must fervently believe, and upon which we must vigorously act. There is no other route to success." — variously attributed to Pablo Picasso, Vincent van Gogh, and Stephen Brennan

You can set the best goals in the world, but without the motivation to work conscientiously toward your goals, you will fail every time. In my case, I only started achieving my goals when I got serious about planning my actions. Before that, all my attempts at achieving my goals quickly sputtered out.

There's actually a psychological reason for this phenomenon. It's fun to dream big.

Setting goals allows you to keep one foot in the realm of fantasy and possibility. In the goal-setting phase, anything can happen. You're just giving a voice to the urges and dreams that have been living inside you. This gives your brain free rein to imagine a beautiful future in which you have everything you ever hoped for. Even if you're following the Turning Point program by writing goals that are on POINT, and thus more constrained by reality, it is easy to fall into the trap of fantasizing about your shiny new life plan.

After you have written down your goals, though, the hard work begins. Even the best-crafted goal begins to fall apart without any concrete action. Now that you have your list of goals, you are officially in the danger zone. Without action, your goals may crumble around you. It's essential to keep your momentum to meet the challenges you have set for yourself. After all, if you don't have to work to achieve something, it's probably not worth doing.

The Power of Writing Down Your Goals

I'm a big believer in the power of words. And when those words are written out on a page, they become even more powerful. Remember that adage about a picture being worth a thousand words? I'll take a detailed, written-down goal over a thousand hypothetical, still-in-the-dreaming-phase goals any day.

A common mistake is to create a flurry of goals, often at the beginning of a new year or a new life phase, without including any way to hold yourself accountable. Writing down your goals provides that accountability. Something about seeing those objectives taken from dreamland and listed clearly on paper makes them much more achievable. Suddenly, everything is more real.

Personally, I am a strong supporter of making your goals look as official as possible. Now is not the time to scribble a few notes on a scrap of notebook paper. (Although, if that's all you have available, go for it!) If you make your goals look official and important, you will treat them as such. Grab some nice paper and neatly type or list your goals. Now, place your list in a place where you will see it often. Whether you stash it in a bedside drawer or proudly attach it to the bathroom mirror, your goals are now impossible to ignore.

I also recommend that you share your goals with a friend or family member. Not only does telling someone about your goals make them more real to you, but it also keeps you accountable. Make sure you choose someone you trust to support you in your goal-achievement journey. If you're not sure whom to tell, the Turning Point forum is a great place to get support and encouragement.

Create a Detailed Action Plan

Now, it's time to turn those goals into reality. Brainstorm all of the steps required to achieve your goal. There might be two steps that need to be repeated over and over, or there may be 40 different steps to reach your objective. Each goal is different; what matters is that you brainstorm all possible routes to achieving the goal as well as any barriers that need to be overcome.

People often say to me, "I think I'm doing something wrong with my action plan. When I look at these, they just seem like boring everyday things." In fact, that's exactly right! Smashing through a big goal is really just a matter of carrying out basic tasks, day after day. The people who keep their motivation along the way are the ones who are unstoppable.

When creating your action steps, remember to be content with incremental progress.

Some days, you will feel full of energy and excitement about your goals. Other days, you might need to drag yourself out of bed to get things done. That's normal. Take my weight loss transformation as an example. After an initial spurt of progress during which I lost a few pounds, I settled into a steady routine. Fat melts away a few ounces at a time, which sometimes makes progress feel agonizingly slow. This is a classic "tortoise beats the hare" situation. Being content with — and even celebrating — incremental progress is critical to your success.

Exercise

Let's walk through some example action plans for a couple of the goals connected to reaching the dream of becoming a best-selling author.

Goal No. 1: I will write at least 500 words per day, five days per week, using time in the morning after the kids go to school.

On its surface, this goal already seems pretty specific. Isn't it just a matter of just sitting down and actually writing 500 words per day? When you think more deeply, though, you should be able to identify concrete steps that will make it much more likely that you will achieve this goal. For example:

1.Create a broad outline for the novel. The details will be filled in as I go along.

2.Brainstorm names for main characters. Write character sketches for each person, so their personalities are established from the beginning of the novel.

3.Inform my partner of my intent to write each morning, so I will not be disturbed during this time.

4.Find a quiet location in which to write.

5.Decorate my writing space with greenery and positive affirmations. This will make it a calm and inviting place for me to write each day.

6.Make sure my laptop is in good working order and I have the extension cord I need to plug it in at my writing desk.

Notice that only a few of these action steps directly pertain to writing itself. The others have to do with creating an environment that is conducive to achieving the goal. It is easy to dismiss these action steps as somehow extraneous to the goal itself. Ultimately, though, they are critical to achieving success. Finding an extension cord and creating an inviting writing space may seem like prosaic details on your way to becoming a best-selling author. Without these things, though, you'll never fulfill your goal of writing 500 words per day.

Therefore, no matter how boring or humdrum you find the action steps, take the time to write them down. Sometimes, goals that seem simple on the surface have hidden variables that you must manage and control through action planning.

Let's take a look at Goal No. 3 and do some more action planning.

Goal No. 3: Within three months, I will become a participant in a fiction writing group in my community.

Steps to achieve this goal might include:

1. Do an Internet search for fiction writing groups in my town.

2. Check Meetup.com for writing groups in my area.

3. Identify the leader of the writing group that best matches my interests.

4. Contact the writing group leader to determine whether the group is accepting new members.

5. If no group is available, do the following:

a. Talk to my friend Melanie, who writes poetry and short fiction. Ask Melanie if she would be interested in creating a writers' workshop with me.

b. Contact Melanie's fellow writer friends to gauge interest.

c. Send out a call on Facebook to see if others in my social circle are interested.

d. Call a first meeting of the group within two weeks.

e. Research common rules for writing groups, including expectations for frequency of writing, constructive criticism, and other guidelines for the group.

f. Create a meeting agenda that includes a workshop calendar.

6. Sign up for a date to present my work to the writing group.

7. Revise two chapters of my novel to present in the writing group.

8. Prepare a short introduction to the concept of my novel, so the group can provide more constructive feedback.

9.Prepare questions to ask the writing group about areas that were effective versus parts that need more work. Take plenty of notes to make this a constructive experience.

Note that this goal requires significantly more direct action steps than Goal No. 1. Furthermore, those steps include a way to overcome a potential barrier that could arise if there are no writing groups in the area. Creating a list of action steps allows you to check items off your list as you pursue your goal. Of course, new barriers may arise that require additional items to be added to the list. With a concrete vision of where you are and where you need to go, these are easier to address as they come up.

Complete Step 1 Within 24 Hours

Here's my most powerful goal achievement secret: Always complete one step toward your goal within the first 24 hours. Now, this doesn't have to be a major step or even the most important step. However, you will achieve so much more if you begin taking action right away. It's just too easy to say, "I'll start for real tomorrow." After a few days of putting off progress toward your goal, it's much less likely that you will ever accomplish your objective. Instead, make the first step happen today.

The first step is often a very easy task, but it is a powerful way to get yourself in a success-oriented mindset. Send an email, research a topic on the Internet, get up an hour earlier in the morning, or walk around the block. These small steps are just the beginning of a whole new approach to your life.

Setting Daily Intentions

Each day, I wake up and review my progress toward my goals. You should do the same. This is when it comes in handy to have your goals in a prominent or easy-to-reach place. It makes it easy to track your progress and hold yourself accountable for your actions each day.

After reviewing my goals, I set intentions for the day. When setting your intentions, remember that on most days, you will be taking little baby steps toward your goal. Some days, you might take a leap forward; other days, you will fall backward. Setting daily intentions keeps your momentum going in a positive direction.

I find that one to three intentions each day is an easy and manageable number. These should be tied directly to your goals. Review your action plan if you're having trouble creating intentions for yourself. For example, an intention might be, "I will ask John to meet me for coffee to discuss options for a career in accounting" or "I will strike up a conversation with a new person at Starbucks" or "I will create a healthy dinner for my family."

These intentions are straightforward, relatively easy to complete, and will keep you engaged with your goals each and every day. But what happens when you start to lose your momentum or fall off your path toward achieving your goals? It's time to talk about troubleshooting barriers to your success.

Barriers to Achieving Your Goals and How to Smash Through Them

Fear of Failure

I list fear of failure first because I believe it to be a primary reason that people do not achieve their goals. We always have excuses about why we didn't obtain the objectives we set for ourselves. When I look back at the previous version of myself, I see someone who cloaked himself in excuses. My constant refrain was, "Well, I would have applied for that job, but I bet they wouldn't want to hire someone like me anyway." Or, "I know that I should stop eating burgers and takeout every day, but I just don't feel up to making healthy food."

The first step is to stop and be honest with yourself. See your excuses for what they are: ways to rationalize your own fear of failing. It's an uncomfortable sensation to embark on

175

a new goal, knowing full well that you might fail spectacularly at it. Blaming external factors for your failures is much easier than admitting that you're at least partially at fault.

Keep in mind that everyone is afraid of failing at the things that are important to them. The more important a goal is to you, the more vulnerable you will feel when going out and chasing it. To conquer that fear, remember that everyone fails. You might fail at the very first goal you set! But as long as you set an on-POINT goal that is well-aligned with your values, you cannot lose. Think of the failure as a minor pitfall in your path toward a more authentic version of yourself. The valleys of failure and frustration make the mountain peaks of success that much sweeter. You'll get there if you believe in your own abilities and self-worth.

Time

When I talk to people, they often cite a lack of time as a reason for failing to follow through on goals. It's true — many of us are busier than ever. However, even the busiest person I know still has time to do the things that are most important to her. She rearranges her schedule to make those things a priority.

If you're feeling strapped for time, start by assessing your daily routine. It may help to write down your activities for each 15-minute increment. Now, look for ways to streamline your life. Behaviors that aren't directly in line with your goals are the first to go. Do you spend 60 minutes every evening watching TV? Perhaps you could sacrifice 30 of those minutes to go for a run. Look for chunks of time throughout the day that could be put to better use.

Loss of Excitement

This is a huge barrier for many people. At some point during the process of working toward your goal, you're going to hit a wall.

You may feel completely unmotivated or even question why you set the goal at all. This is when it's most important to revisit your values. These are the true reasons that you're reaching for the goal. Reconnecting to what is most important to you is a great way to feel reinvigorated about your goals.

Sometimes, though, you just need to get out of a rut. Have you been dutifully writing your 500 words each day from your desk at home? Hop over to a coffee shop for a change of scenery! Treat yourself to a new brand of tea! Anything that shakes up your usual routine can bring back your excitement.

People Who Get in Your Way

Without realizing it, you may have surrounded yourself with people who have a negative mindset or keep you stuck in bad patterns. This is very common, particularly if you are dealing with depression or anxiety. Having a negative approach toward life attracts other people with similarly negative outlooks.

Learn to recognize people who negatively affect your ability to achieve your goals. They are the ones who question your abilities, encourage you to stay home, or pull you into their own bad habits. It's time to gradually limit your time with these people. Instead, cultivate the relationships that make you feel good about yourself. Ask yourself, "If I tell this person that I achieved my goal, what will she say?" Surround yourself with people who would enthusiastically and honestly celebrate your successes. Avoid those who would be consumed with jealousy, question your progress, or make snide remarks.

An "I'll Never Make It" Attitude

Questioning your progress toward a goal is normal. But if you're constantly moaning that you'll never make it to your goal, it's time to reframe your thoughts. This is the perfect time for a "fake it till you make it" moment. Even if you don't feel the internal motivation, act like someone who is confident in his or her ability to accomplish a goal. Soon, you'll internalize this attitude and truly become the person who topples that first goal.

So You've Accomplished a Goal. Now What?

Congratulations! You've conquered your first goal. It's time to stop and celebrate your accomplishment. Then, you're ready to figure out what to tackle next.

Even if the goal seems small to you — for example, "to foster my creativity by taking a painting class" — it's a big reason to celebrate. People who celebrate their accomplishments are much more likely to maintain momentum on their positive life trajectories. Figure out a celebration that feels authentic to you. Share your big accomplishment with a friend. Treat yourself to a pedicure. Go out to dinner with your partner, or make a fancy dinner at home. Buy something you've had your eye on.

After you've celebrated, take a critical look at what was involved in achieving that goal. Note the factors that kept you motivated to succeed. It will be crucial to promote those factors when creating an action plan for your next goal. Also think about the barriers that popped up in your way. Consider how you overcame them and what you might do differently next time. Reflecting on the experience of achieving your goal not only solidifies your accomplishment, but it also reinforces good habits. This will give you the momentum to propel you toward the next goal on your list.

Now, revisit your values list. Think back to where you were before. Is your life more in line with your values? How does that make you feel? Consider some next steps that can bring you even closer to the things that are most important in your life.

Life is long, and we're never done learning or achieving new things. Following the Turning Point steps truly transformed my life in ways that I never could have imagined. You, too, can share in this success by working through the phases, setting great goals, and crafting a new life that is true to your values.

Turning Point: Relationships

"A deep sense of love and belonging is an irreducible need of all people. We are biologically, cognitively, physically, and spiritually wired to love, to be loved and to belong. When those needs are not met, we don't function as we were meant to. We break. We fall apart. We numb. We ache. We hurt others. We get sick."[1]

— Brené Brown, research professor at University of Houston Graduate College of Social Work

Brown's rather poetic summation of the significance of relationships in our lives strikes a chord. If you are anything like me — in other words, if you are human — you, too, can probably relate all too well to the need to belong. Never seeming to belong was a constant state for me during my adolescence.

Since you made the choice to pick up this book, I'm guessing that something is out of whack in your life. And if your life isn't going as well as you'd like, my bet is that your relationships aren't either, and you could probably use some help in this area.

Aaron Rentfrew

The Makings of Self-Esteem

Regardless of your good intentions, does it seem that something always causes you to screw up your interpersonal relationships? Do you often change things about yourself just to fit in and still end up uninvited to the party or not really feeling connected? Are you constantly haunted by the feeling that you are too awkward, too affectionate, too withdrawn, too afraid, or too worrisome? I have dealt with all of these issues in my own life.

"WE RISE BY LIFTING OTHERS"
-ROBERT INGERSOLL

The "too much of this" or "never enough of that" syndrome that we frequently find ourselves fighting stems from low self-esteem. Throughout our lives, particularly in childhood but continuing through adolescence and beyond, we form opinions and beliefs about who we are. Each and every experience provides us with more messages, which we use to reinforce our beliefs about ourselves.

If you have had an overwhelming amount of bad experiences in your life, your beliefs about your worthiness and goodness may be negative, too.

A lot of these formative experiences occur early in life. Maybe you were neglected or abused as a child and never felt secure love from your parents or family. Maybe your parents had really high standards, and the bar moved further away each time you got close to grasping it. Maybe you had trouble either academically or behaviorally, and no one ever took the time to offer you support. Maybe you were picked on by older siblings or kids at school. Maybe no one ever had anything good to say about you but only criticized you for your wrongdoing. Experiences such as these can contribute to the construction of a poor foundation for your sense of self.

All humans have basic needs, including safety, love, attention, affirmation, and belonging. As we age, we learn that we have some level of control over whether these needs are met. When they aren't, we start to develop explanations for why.

For instance, let's say you invite a kid at school to play video games over at your house on the weekend. He turns you down, saying he's busy. You assume that his rejection of you is your fault — you aren't interesting enough, or your video games aren't the newest versions. But it's entirely possible that the kid really has another obligation. But because of what you've told yourself about this rejection, over time, you come to blame your lack of friends on yourself — your boring personality or lack of charm. From there, your journey toward self-hatred and destructive relationships begins.

Are you tired of feeling this way? Are you officially done with believing that you are too much of one thing or not enough of another? Are you ready to take action and enjoy the rewards that come with having satisfying relationships?

Good, because there's something you can do about it. You can learn to love and accept yourself for who you are, overriding those negative messages that have kept you stuck in dissatisfaction. You can learn to identify common snags that may stand in the way of your having healthy relationships and adopt strategies to overcome those snags.

Let's dive in!

The Power of Personal Relationships

"I don't need anyone" is one of the biggest lies you can ever tell yourself.

Relationships are the cornerstones of our lives, and frequently, we find that it is through our connections with others that we feel truly alive. When we have good news, we instantly think about whom we'd like to share it with. When we are lonely, a spontaneous phone call or a visit from a loved one can lift our spirits and help us feel not so alone. Our laughter and joy is magnified in the presence of others. Sorrow is lessened.

I'll sum up the secret to good relationships in three words: They take work.

Despite all the nurturing, apologies, compromises, and sacrifices that they require, fulfilling relationships are so very worth it. Research has shown that strong social ties work much the same as the ambrosia of ancient Greek mythology, bestowing a longer life on all who partake. One study showed that having strong relationships decreased the risk of premature death by 50 percent!

If that's not convincing enough, healthy relationships also help us to effectively manage stress, fight illness, and boost our well-being. On the flip side, being socially isolated can lead to a long list of unwelcome side effects, including lower immune functioning, depression, and hypertension.

As I shared earlier in this book, I started out with less than satisfactory relationships, never feeling as if I belonged. And I suffered from health issues, which I now realize were at least in part related to my social isolation. By following the Turning Point system, I was able to make incredible positive changes in myself that eventually led to improved social connections, as well. It's a good thing you're reading, because the same thing can happen for you. You just need to know where to start.

Family

To make true and sustainable changes in your relationships, you have to go back to the drawing board. For humans, that proverbial drawing board is our families. The only way we can thoroughly examine our relationships and deconstruct our interpersonal issues is to understand their roots.

So you're going to have to revisit your early familial experiences to discover the patterns that have carried over into your adult life. This deconstruction is essential in order for you to reconstruct your life with meaningful and healthy relationships.

Think of it as a complex math problem where your answer doesn't come out quite right. You have to go back to the very first step and then examine each part of the process to see where you went wrong. That's the only way you can correct your mistake and find the right answer. What you're going to do here is similar. But you are not — I repeat, *not* — going back to the drawing board to point the finger and assign blame.

Blaming your parents, grandparents, siblings, uncles, aunts, or cousins for problems in your current relationships is unhelpful. Even if someone did something particularly horrible to you, you have to consider the possibility that this dysfunction was passed along from a previous generation.

It's important to avoid blame at all costs. Blame takes away your power and makes you weak. When you point the finger toward others as the cause of your discontentment, you take the focus off the internal issue. You might succeed in making the other person feel guilty; you might even get a sincere apology. But you won't have done any healing or growing internally. This book is about taking action. And only by refocusing on your internal issues can you act to change the circumstances.

For example, my parents divorcing had a huge impact on my outlook about relationships for more years than I can count. Initially, I internalized what happened between my parents and used it as a frame of reference for every relationship I entered. Without a doubt, I blamed myself along with them for their breakup and for my own relationship failures, as well. Eventually, though, as I worked through the Turning Point phases, I saw the situation more clearly. My parents separated because they were incompatible, not because there was something wrong with me. Understanding this helped me see my own relationships differently, too.

To rebuild and strengthen your existing interpersonal relationships, take a good look at some of the foundational moments in your childhood and adolescence that involved your family. Think about what beliefs, thoughts, worries, prejudices, and dreams you developed due to these primary relationships.

Revisit the assumptions you formed about relationships during your childhood. Does anything strike you differently now that you look at things through an older, more mature lens? Without blaming anyone, think about what may have contributed to some of your relationship problems. Can you spot patterns across different relationships that may have been affected by your views?

Romantic Relationships

Romantic love: Many artists devote their entire careers trying to understand and depict it. It's a feeling that most people long for above all others. It's also a term that can prompt a fearful person to run for the hills.

When our romantic relationships are running smoothly, there's not a cloud in the sky.

When things are rocky, the clouds are overcast and gloomy.

What's really frustrating is when we get in our own way in our relationships. Ideas and opinions we have had growing up override our brains and push us to say and do things we later regret. We hurt inwardly about something, and we take the pain out on our partners. We expect our partners to meet some perfect ideal that we have constructed, and when they show us that they, too, are only human, we can't handle it. We fight to protect our pride and prove our partners wrong rather than to reach agreement. We look for partners to complete us as though we are not whole on our own.

Thriving romantic relationships are very possible. But they take commitment, work, and continuous awareness. Such relationships require two emotionally whole individuals who work together to overcome challenges. We will learn more about the most common relationship challenges and how to counteract them in just a moment.

Friendships

As we get older and our responsibilities multiply, we often realize the difficulty of maintaining old friendships and developing new connections. Work, child-rearing, relocating, and caring for elderly parents can all throw a wrench in our social lives. Months or years may pass, and suddenly you notice yourself wondering, "Whatever happened to…?"

Sadly, our friendships often drop down the priority list when life gets hectic. But they shouldn't. When you are unattached to a romantic partner, friendships can provide you with companionship to prevent loneliness. Our friends also serve as sources of support during tough times; they enhance our sense of belonging, boost our self-confidence, and help us fight stress.

With all those benefits, an investment of time and effort into building and maintaining friendships is certainly worthwhile. Are you wondering how to invest in your friendships? These relationships are nurtured in the same way as other interpersonal relationships. Keep reading to learn how to improve all of your relationships.

Professional Relationships

People who have a buddy on the job are seven times as likely to be engaged in their work, according to a Gallup report. Fostering relationships at work can improve employee satisfaction by 50 percent. When you have a close friend at work, you receive the advantages of sharing a purpose with the team, you have someone on whom you can rely, and you've got a source of support or someone to listen to you vent on bad days.

We are social creatures by nature. When we can link our employment with socialization, our work lives become more enjoyable. Plus, forming connections at work allows us to become better at what we do. When we take the time to personally know the people with whom we work, our performance and productivity improve. The "I" mentality recedes in favor of the "we" mentality.

Are you having trouble developing your professional relationships? Learning how to overcome the major hurdles can significantly improve your satisfaction at work.

Overcoming the Disconnect

Improving your relationships involves a two-part process of acceptance and action. To have thriving relationships, something about what you're doing right now needs to change. Later, we will discuss some of the larger obstacles that may stand in the way of enjoying fulfilling relationships. These hurdles require a level of awareness of what could be working against you in your relationships followed by mindful action to overcome these hurdles.

Before we get into that, I want to point out that one of the most subtle relationship issues we humans face time and time again is failing to accept who we are. When we persist in our childhood beliefs that we are unworthy or not good enough, those beliefs are strengthened, and they stand in the way of our happiness. It's time to learn self-acceptance.

Self-Acceptance

As I've said before, you're going to have to make some changes if you want to claim your innate power and stamp out the behaviors that have been hindering your progress toward living the life you want. But changing yourself completely to fit in will only leave you feeling frustrated and unsatisfied. Some parts of ourselves — our interests, our dreams, our quirks — are what make us feel alive. If you were to eliminate these parts, you wouldn't be yourself anymore. You'd be an actor who changes character depending on the audience. Does that sound satisfying — or draining?

Most of my life, I fought a hard battle to try to fit in. My guess is, since you're reading this, that you probably have, too.

I'm here to tell you that you shouldn't be trying to fit in. What's more important is feeling like you *belong*.

According to researcher Brené Brown, we often assume that fitting in and belonging mean the same thing. They don't. Fitting in is an attempt to change yourself to accommodate others. Belonging involves the courageous act of showing up and letting yourself be seen for who you really are.

The only way you can gain a sense of belonging is to first accept who you are. Once you believe that who you are is enough, you can be fully present in your relationships.

One way to improve your relationships — and your life — is by working exclusively on your self-esteem, since it plays a large role in how you view yourself. Self-esteem work often involves focusing on the better parts of who you are. But humans are neither all good nor all bad. When you focus instead on self-acceptance, you learn to embrace the positive *and* negative parts of yourself. It's an unconditional welcoming of your core self without making judgments of "good" or "bad."

Now, let's be clear: Self-acceptance isn't about letting yourself off easy or being complacent. Instead, it means dropping the habit of beating yourself up and criticizing your imperfections. You can practice self-acceptance by doing the following:

- Release the need to demonstrate your worth to others or get their approval.

- Look at all that you have to offer the world and the people in it.
- View yourself as deserving and worthy of love and belonging.
- Be willing to confront the parts of yourself you find unacceptable.
- Acknowledge that withholding goodwill from yourself also prevents you from fully extending it to others.
- Challenge your self-criticisms. How accurate are they? If you find yourself saying, "I'm not good enough," look for instances where you have surpassed the standard and been more than enough.
- Recognize that you are human and imperfect. You are doing the best you can.
- Forgive yourself, and try to make amends for past transgressions, if possible.

By nurturing an attitude of self-acceptance, you give yourself the freedom to be all right without changing a single thing. Of course, positive change is the ultimate goal with the Turning Point. Still, you have to overcome the idea that you can never be worthy unless you meet certain criteria. Self-acceptance allows you to be enough as you are, even in the midst of a major self-improvement undertaking such as this. As your self-acceptance increases, so too will your sense of belonging, because you will no longer be fighting or tweaking your quirks in a counterproductive attempt to fit in.

Major Relationship Hurdles

We all want to be happier, more connected, more forgiving, and more caring to those around us. We all want to live the good life, and creating solid, fulfilling relationships is a major part of that. Hopefully, by now, you have found a measure of self-acceptance for who you naturally are without feeling the need to fit in.

Getting to a place of self-acceptance is extremely powerful. Once you are there, you can honestly assess your past behavior in relationships and identify methods to improve it going forward. These are not strategies you'll be able to adopt overnight. These are huge undertakings that may take you weeks, months, or even years to master. But as long as you have come to a place of self-acceptance, you won't criticize yourself for slow progress. Don't forget, slow and steady wins the race.

In the next sections, I'll go over some of the main issues that tend to damage relationships, hindering their growth and making them more difficult to maintain.

Great (or Not-So-Great) Expectations

A wise person once said, "What screws us up most in life is the picture in our head of how it is supposed to be." I'm not sure who first expressed this insightful sentiment, but the message is clear: Be careful of your expectations.

Picture this: You meet an interesting person, Chris, at your local coffee shop. You two really hit it off, and you decide to exchange phone numbers. You wait for a call — one day, then two. You overanalyze the meeting, questioning Chris' behavior and your own. You tell yourself, "I knew it was too good to be true. Chris didn't even really like me." You beat yourself up for another day. On the fourth day, Chris calls and asks you out for dinner. Over dinner, Chris expresses a great liking for you but is worried about rushing into things too soon after a breakup. Chris asks if it's OK to take things slow.

High expectations in the above scenario could have completely jeopardized a budding relationship and could have led you to being resistant to dating in the future.

Even outside of dating relationships, our expectations are often unreasonable. With our family members, best friends, and co-workers, unrealistically high expectations tend to result in disappointment after disappointment.

Don't get me wrong; there's plenty of research that confirms having high expectations can lead to greater satisfaction and motivation. This very well may be true in terms of work, school, or personal goal attainment. If setting the bar high pushes you to work harder, and this is working for you, by all means, carry on.

However, when it comes to others, having unrealistically high expectations just leads to a doomed relationship. Once you start to criticize and judge those around you for not hitting the mark, it eventually seems like everyone you meet is letting you down.

Adjusting your expectations is a very active process. Why? Because your expectations of others are usually strengthened by previous experience. People tend to use "confirmation bias" to support their expectations. The reasoning goes like this: "My spouse/friend/parent has let me down tons of times in the past. The same thing will probably happen in the future."

You can overcome this natural tendency toward confirmation bias by challenging yourself to carefully examine each situation for how it is unique from previous ones. This technique prevents you from expecting the worst by first questioning how your assumption might be wrong.

For example, let's say your business partner shows up late to a marketing event and says it's because he had a disagreement with his wife. You're all ready to relieve him of his duties or chastise him for being late. He did the same thing two weeks ago. Only that time, he was late because he had to pick his son up from the dentist. So while similar, these two scenarios are not exactly the same. Recognizing the minor differences can be just enough to stop you from bowling head-first into an expectations trap. Perhaps your colleague is having a difficult time in his home life and really needs your patience and understanding.

Shaming others for being human and making mistakes is rarely helpful in building long-lasting relationships. Compassion is. Therefore, instead of expecting too much from loved ones, try to slightly lower your expectations of them and raise your expectations of yourself. This isn't intended to promote stagnancy or toxic relationships. It's intended to be freeing. When you take this approach, your loved one is free to be who he or she naturally is without being subject to your expectations. You, in turn, are freed from constant disappointment.

Try giving more of yourself. Offer help, nurturing, and support to others without any expectation of compensation. Then, when you do get more from others than you expect, you will be pleasantly surprised.

Communication

Many people will tell you that virtually all relationship problems arise from failed communication. I agree. It doesn't matter if you are just meeting a new friend or trying to keep the flame going in your marriage. In order for any sort of relationship to be successful, effective communication is a must.

There are a range of ways the communication lines can be broken in your interpersonal relationships. You are undecided about how you feel on a topic, so you blurt out something offensive to a friend who has a strong opinion. You're more focused on checking your social media accounts than holding a conversation with your boyfriend. Instead of saying "Good morning" to your co-worker, you start right in on the error he made on a report. You suffer in silence, not telling your parents about a health problem, because your family doesn't usually discuss personal topics.

In addition to these common examples of broken communication, the steady increase in the use of smartphones and social media has built up a huge wall in the communication department. Many friends, families, and couples find themselves constantly vying for one another's attention against Facebook, LinkedIn, or Pinterest. Knowing that the odds are not in your favor means you have to work extra hard to prevent miscommunication. The next few sections discuss some strategies you can implement to achieve better communication in all of your relationships.

Active Listening

One main reason we struggle to communicate is that many of us listen to respond instead of listening to understand.

Try to actively listen to your conversation partner by doing the following:

- Listen without interruption.
- Demonstrate engagement by facing the speaker directly and making eye contact. It can also be helpful to nod or make appropriate facial expressions in response to the speaker's message.
- React. Paraphrase what the other person has said to show understanding. You might say something like, "It sounds like you're saying…"
- Show empathy. Acknowledge what the speaker is feeling by responding to the emotional part of the message. You might say, "It seems like you are very upset about this situation."
- Avoid judgment. Refrain from invalidating the speaker or offering a counterargument.
- Save the advice. Don't rush the conversation by jumping too quickly into the problem-solving phase. If it is

solicited, present your advice after the other's perspective has been completely conveyed.

Being Direct

Another challenge to successful communication is the act of beating around the bush. I can't tell you how much I dread the four words, "We need to talk." Slow-dancing your way into a difficult conversation doesn't make it any less difficult. Instead, it causes the receiver's mind to wander right off a cliff. When a person hears those four words, it causes a sinking feeling. It's like a red flag waving with the words, "Trouble ahead."

When you are indirect about expressing your feelings or concerns, you give the other person time to get defensive, which is a surefire way to kill a productive conversation. A more effective strategy is to be open, honest, and straightforward. Use "I" statements to show ownership and acceptance of your thoughts and feelings while minimizing the other's likelihood of becoming defensive.

For example, try starting your conversation by saying something like this: "I feel ignored when you stare at your phone when I'm talking. I would appreciate it if you could look at me when I speak." That type of statement is much more likely to be received amicably than something accusatory such as, "You always ignore me when I talk."

Recognizing When It Can't Be Fixed

There are times when no amount of work can save a relationship. Some relationships simply are not meant to be; some people are naturally unsuited to one another. You will be wiser and better if you recognize this fact rather than sacrificing your health and well-being by staying in an unfixable relationship.

Whether the relationship involves a family member, friend, romantic partner, or co-worker, here are a few signs that the connection is toxic and that it's best to get some distance:

- Your self-esteem suffers in the person's presence.
- You notice yourself acting in ways that do not align with your personal values.
- You self-medicate with alcohol or drugs or cope in other unhealthy ways to handle the person's presence in your life.
- You are always complaining about the person to others.
- You never look forward to seeing this person.
- You find it hard to take responsibility for your actions and blame this person for your behavior.
- Your other relationships are taking a nosedive because of this person's presence in your life.

- Your personal boundaries are not being upheld or respected in the relationship.

Moving Forward

Making use of the tips outlined here should allow you to make progress in your interpersonal relationships. Striving for self-acceptance, adjusting your expectations, and overcoming communication barriers can help improve your relationship satisfaction by leaps and bounds. However, you must also be prepared to terminate relationships that are not serving you. If you are in a relationship that is keeping you in your old ways or preventing you from living the life you want to have, you need to make the decision to walk away.

After working through the four phases of the Turning Point, you should find it easier to take the steps needed to revitalize your existing relationships and build strong, healthy new ones. This in turn will do wonders for bettering your life overall. It's a cycle of continuous improvement that will bring you benefits far beyond the effort you put in to make it happen.

---

[1] Brown, Brené, Want to be happy? Stop trying to be perfect, CNN.com,

http://www.cnn.com/2010/LIVING/11/01/give.up.perfection/

Turning Point: New Normal

Few things have turned society on its head like social media. Since the launch of MySpace in early 2004, we've been hooked. And there are some good reasons for that. Understanding the dynamics of social media and how it effects our frame of mind is becoming more and more important as we spend an increasing amount of time absorbed by it.

Social Media:
The Good, the Bad, and the Ugly

At first, social media pulled us in with the promise of reconnecting us with high school classmates and distant relatives. At the same time, we discovered that we could also obsessively lurk as well as ogle and follow the lives of our "friends" in snapshots from afar, gleaning information from hashtags like #isaidyes and #babymatthewscomingsoon. We also found ourselves soaking up every posted and tweeted opinion about matters both serious and trivial.

Social media is the source by which many of us get our news about the world at large. One commonly quoted statistic says that more than half of all Americans learn about breaking news via social media. This includes everything from local traffic accidents to school shootings and political updates.

The proliferation of social networks has been influential in getting people more involved with politics, helping them spread awareness about important causes and beliefs, inciting social change, assisting job seekers to find employment, bridging the gap between businesses and their customers, and improving everyone's knowledge and use of technology.

In many ways, social media has made the world smaller and more connected. Yet there are also vast disadvantages to the social media vortex that has sucked us all in.

Once upon a time, you'd have to ring a girl's landline and cringe as her father gruffly answered the phone and demanded to know everything about you since your family settled in this country. Just over a decade and a half ago, you simply had to wait to hear back from someone by phone because, at that time, even email was used infrequently.

These days, it's hardly that simple. One of the biggest downsides of social media is how it has changed the way we communicate. You can get in touch with someone in countless ways beyond email and telephone. Within the social networks themselves, there are a multitude of options: text messages, video messages, video calls, chatting, and the list goes on.

Are all these methods of communication actually connecting us? Yes — and no.

We have more "friends" but less contact — greater reach but less voice. We have never been more connected to people, but we are simultaneously deprived of *feeling* a connection. The strength of our connections with others is often dependent on the level of our phone battery and our proximity to an electrical outlet.

Social media feeds are customized to deliver nonstop information about our passions and interests, dragging us further and further from center. We see everyone's "highlight reel" moments as we scroll down the news feed, yet we are unable to look people in the eye and notice when they are feeling down. Family connections, while more frequent, are just as unfulfilling.

Imagine a wolf pack. Its members hunt together, support one another, and maintain a social structure. As a pack, they flourish. The lone wolf typically struggles, starves, and is far less likely to survive the severe weather. The more we use social media, the further we retreat into our lonely wolf selves. *Together, we are alone.*

Thanks to the creation of social media platforms, our range of connection is no longer limited by those we can meet in person or connect with through mutual acquaintances. We now have access to virtually everyone else on the planet who also happens to have Internet access, which is currently more than 3.3 billion people. Considering this huge number — more than 45 percent of the world's population — it's no wonder it has become incredibly common to have thousands of Facebook friends or Instagram and Twitter followers.

Do we personally know all these people? Of course not. But who cares? Everybody's doing it. If I happen to sound like a wisecracking teenager, that's telling, as well.

The pervasiveness of social media has regressed our social skills back to adolescence.

In a blind rage, we log onto one among dozens of social networking sites and vent our despairs to our friends or followers. These same online rants have the potential to ruin job opportunities and romantic relationships.

All of this happens in mere seconds — practically instantaneously. And this is what we call the "new normal."

Beyond the number of people to whom we now have access at any given moment, technological advancements have also affected how we interact and how we feel about ourselves in the process.

We can spend hours or days catching up on every tiny detail in others' lives while doing very little to improve our own. We catch the highlights of our friends' days and inwardly beat ourselves up for not taking better selfies, for not achieving those super-toned abs, for not going further in school, or for not being a perfect parent or a perfect spouse.

When it comes to social media, we are constantly pulled in, but more times than we'd like, what we get is a great big sinking feeling of inadequacy. It's not surprising. After all, what are you doing? You're lying on your couch scrolling through your Facebook feed while you binge-watch Netflix on a Saturday night while your friends are in their best threads partying it up in the city — at least according to Facebook. Such minute life comparisons make it all too easy to think to yourself, "My life sucks."

Such constant comparisons of our own lives with those of our peers, made possible by social media usage, have been linked by researchers with mental health issues such as poor self-esteem, depression, and loneliness. What's more, scientists have determined that when social media use causes envy, depressive symptoms are more likely to crop up. That means when you're logging onto Facebook to size up how well Mike's marriage is going or which exotic vacation he's jetting off to now, you could be opening yourself up to depression.

But here's the thing: The inadequacies we feel from scrolling down our timelines and news feeds are terribly misplaced. A great analogy developed by the online therapy site Talkspace is of a carnival fun house. When you walk inside, everywhere you look, the images reflected back to you are distorted versions of themselves. You may look taller, shorter, thinner, or fatter. These houses of mirrors are constructed to humor you with their misleading representations of you and your surroundings.

Social media produces the same effect. It is reality — but distorted.

But when it comes to social media, what you see may not always humor you; instead, it may make you feel lesser than or just not enough.

Like the carnival fun house, social media does not give you an accurate reflection of real life. You see a photo or update of a very small slice of another person's life — a representation of that person's "online self." As a casual observer, you have no idea what happens to that friend an hour after that photo or status is posted. You have no clue what filters were used — literally and metaphorically — to deliver the final image.

This leaves you making unfair comparisons. When you enter a carnival fun house filled with tricky mirrors, you go in knowing how you really look. So the reflections, no matter how real they may seem, are nevertheless clearly distortions. However, when you log on to Facebook or Instagram and see snapshots of a classmate's life, those images may be the only version of your friend's life that you ever see. There's no way to easily tell how closely they reflect reality.

In the world of social networking, an important rule of thumb is to remember that not everything you see, hear, or read is exactly as it seems.

Taking a Closer Look

I'm sure you're probably wondering what all this has to do with improving yourself. Your first impression may be that I'm a proponent of the anti-social media movement. Perhaps you expect me to get on my soapbox to tell you how Facebook and Instagram are saturating every part of your life and plead with you to save yourself while you can. I'm not going to do that.

What I am going to do is show you the astounding effects that social media has on every part of your life, from your work to your relationships. These effects are not necessarily all good or all bad.

In Phases 1 through 4 of the program, I directed you to the Turning Point forum to share your personal story with others for support and as testimony to help others grow. I believe that the social aspects of the Internet allow us to connect and engage with like-minded people who may be on similar journeys to our own. At the same time, though, I must point out how the use of social media disconnects and disengages us, too. Fortunately, recognizing the problem is also the first step in solving it.

As with most things, social media can act as both a blessing and a curse. So what we're going to do together is take a closer look at some of the potential downsides to these sites and discuss how they can deter you from becoming the person you ideally want to be.

After we've identified the ways that social media can interfere with the positive change process — as well as the maintenance required after changing — I'll go over some useful strategies you can use to try to minimize the negative impact of social media on your life and your growth.

Before we begin, let me say that I understand your frustration. You may be tempted to skip past this part. You might truly believe that this new normal isn't affecting you at all. Even if you don't use social media excessively, chances are that if someone around you does, it's having some sort of effect on you. Because of how stealthily social media has crept into nearly every facet of our lives, these issues can be hard to spot. But that doesn't mean they're not there.

So, once again, let's get truthful. The following sections explore how social media affects us in various aspects of our lives and the challenges that it presents.

Interpersonal Relationships

Effects of a Mobile Nation

We laugh ourselves silly at a meme of a distracted woman checking her social media account and walking into a pole, but such a scenario is hardly far-fetched in today's social media-addicted world. Want proof? The next time you are standing in line waiting somewhere or are attending a social gathering, count the percentage of those around you who are engrossed with their smartphones. Chances are, most of them are on some sort of social networking site. Facebook remains the most popular, with 62 percent of American adults and 71 percent of teens using the site.

Challenges

Online social media outlets such as Facebook can provoke turmoil within romantic relationships. It seems the more times you log on and post, the more likely it is that your significant other will start to get jealous, which can stimulate even greater relationship problems.

Even when we are offline, our relationships can be negatively affected by social media. Losing oneself in a smartphone or other device to connect with the online world has left people severely disconnected with the physical world. We now have less practice carrying out real, face-to-face conversations. Plus, an excess of online friends requires so much attention and maintenance that we have little time left to meet new people and have fulfilling relationships that are not reliant on an Internet connection.

Sadly, families aren't exempt from the impact of social media. Long gone are the days of healthy conversation during mealtimes unless parents are extra careful about banning smartphones from the dinner table. Studies show that being immersed in such media can interfere with a family's interpersonal bonding.

Aaron Rentfrew

Work and Leadership

Effects of a Mobile Nation

Today's highly connected world often negatively affects our professional lives, causing a major disconnect between leaders and their teams. In a 2001 Harvard Business School *Bulletin* article, various professors weighed in on the qualities that make a good leader; they all agreed that *communication is a key element.*

Leaders must be able to convey difficult topics with ease and simplicity. They must closely understand their teams and the individual professionals within those teams in order to engage, motivate, and inspire in a way that resonates with everyone. The problem with this in today's workplace is that an overwhelming amount of communication is conducted via email.

Further complicating the communication issue, more and more workers are now telecommuting. As a result, those who lead must make drastic changes in the way they supervise, coordinate, and motivate their teams. It's quite common today for employees and their leaders to be cities or oceans apart, forcing them to connect via phone, email, or social communication sites such as Google Hangouts or Skype.

Challenges

An email-centric workplace is the breeding ground for a disconnected leader. Crafting an informative email updating the team on projects and numbers is all good, but to truly influence employees, reinforce objectives, and boost morale, leaders must come out from behind the desk and, on occasion, deliver their messages face-to-face.

Cultural and language barriers also undermine the effectiveness of communicating via email. An American, for example, would most likely communicate much more directly about a problem than an

Asian might. As a result, conflict and misunderstanding can divide the team and create distrust issues that impede performance and productivity.

Furthermore, when email or other disconnected forms of communication are used, employees receiving the messages can only perceive what is right in front of them. When team members communicate over the phone or via email, they are challenged to discern one another's messages without the help of nonverbal clues such as body language and facial expressions. Occasional face-to-face contact can overcome these barriers.

For instance, a Gallup study shows that when managers hold regular meetings with their teams, employees are three times as likely to be engaged in their work than those on teams that do not meet regularly. The same research further demonstrates that the leaders who use a combination of communication methods, such as phone, email, videoconferencing, and in-person meetings, are most effective of all.

Email is most helpful for scheduling and confirming tasks or meetings. The telephone or videoconferencing may be fine for quick two-way discussions. However, in-person meetings are optimal for honest dialogue, brainstorming sessions, and reaching mutual agreement.

Personal Growth

Effects of a Mobile Nation

The proliferation of social media networks has increased the impact that people online can have in our personal lives, especially in the form of mentoring. Although not an entirely new concept, online mentoring — or "e-mentoring" — is now a growing trend.

Whether used for career, educational, or personal development reasons, online mentoring gives mentors and mentees the ability to connect while overcoming the usual obstacles in mentoring relationships, such as gender, race, hierarchy, and age. Mentors may "meet" with interested mentees through online messaging systems, via video calls, or through webinars in which multiple mentees are present at once.

Challenges

Despite the positive aspects of mentees being able to receive impartial advice from mentors all over the world, there are some drawbacks to this personal growth product. For one, as with many forms of communication carried out from afar, online mentoring leaves much room for miscommunication. The language style of each participant may undermine the budding closeness of the relationship, which proves that quality matching between mentor and mentee is essential.

In addition, research shows that e-mentoring leads to much slower relationship development. An online mentoring relationship is a weak tie; it involves fewer communications, a more narrow focus, and more superficial bonds. But it is through strong relationship ties, such as those that are formed face-to-face, that better social and psychological outcomes emerge.

Unlike face-to-face mentoring relationships, online mentoring relationships don't give mentees the chance to watch their mentors model the behaviors they promote. This lack of real role modeling can lead to less commitment from mentees over time. Moreover, face-to-face meetings tend to involve more planning and preparation, and the mentee gets the mentor's undivided attention for a span of time. When engaging virtually, the mentor may send an immediate response via email or messaging but could also be juggling mentoring with other work tasks and therefore providing a subpar experience for the mentee.

Summing It Up

So far, we have discussed the potential benefits and drawbacks of social media on our lives. In terms of self-improvement, it's not an exaggeration to say that your social media use has the power to make or break you. Here's a review of what we've covered:

- Social media allows us more connections, yet they are more shallow in nature.
- Social media use can result in poor self-esteem, anxiety, and depression, among other concerns.
- Our "friends" present snapshots of their lives for us to view —and possibly envy — but these snapshots are only fragments of the whole, and as such, frequently give us a distorted impression of reality.
- Social media use can have detrimental impacts on romantic relationships, the ability to form new friendships, and family bonds.

- Productivity and engagement at work can be jeopardized when leaders count on email to communicate with their teams.
- Online mentoring relationships tend not to be as strong or effective as those conducted in person.

Now that you've had a chance to consider the issue in some depth, you may be wondering what you can or should do about it. That's what we're going to tackle next.

Balancing the New Normal

By now, you should have a thorough understanding of the pitfalls of social media. You may even be getting ready to swear off social media for good. Taking such an extreme approach may work for some, but for others, completely cutting out social media use is out of the question. And you don't have to give it up. A *careful* balance of social media use can result in richer online and offline relationships, a productive professional life, and greater personal growth, all while protecting the stability of your mental health and well-being.

How can you achieve this? You must take strides to make your social interactions work for you instead of against you. You must take purposeful steps to shield yourself from the known pitfalls by engaging in more mindful and less destructive Internet and social networking use. This can be accomplished through five important measures. Let's go through them one at a time.

Awareness

I have said it time and time again, and that's because it's true: Change happens when we look at our problems head-on. It's what the Turning Point is all about —deconstructing your issues so you can reconstruct a truly fulfilling life. Living well amidst the new normal works in much the same way. To counteract the effects of pervasive social media, you have to let go of the "everybody else is doing it" excuse and look at the issue for what it is.

Remember, recognizing the problem is the first step toward implementing a solution, and as the saying goes, when we know better, we do better. After reading about the many ways social media can affect your life, both positively and negatively, you should have some idea of the true power of these tools in your life. Are you happy with this power? Is your social networking use meaningful and positive? Or is it time-draining, envy-producing, or otherwise less than desirable?

If the information I've presented here has shown you that social media has too much power in your life and is hindering your path to success, then you need to take back that power and create a desirable relationship with social media.

If your social media use is not at all limiting in your life, then by all means pat yourself on the back; you're one of a rare breed. Still, exploring the rest of these balancing measures may be beneficial to you when you interact with others who misuse social tools.

Extra Effort

Finding successful balance means putting in a little extra time and effort to spot undesirable behavior patterns and overcome them. This means being conscious of envy and reminding yourself that, just like you, your Facebook friends have ups and downs in their lives that may not make it to their status posts. Don't take their lives at face value, and you'll have a much healthier perspective.

Expending extra effort also means taking the time to truly cherish the people and experiences you enjoy offline. Going into zombie mode with your phone while out with friends sends the message that whatever you're looking at online is more important than the people in the room with you. Put the phone down and absorb some real life.

Rather than rushing to document every single moment of a birthday party or cross-country trip, designate a specific time of day to log on and update your followers about your activities. That way you'll have more intimacy in the moment, because your entire friends list won't be watching your every cocktail and meal.

Golden Rule in Reverse

Many people are familiar with the idea of treating others the way they themselves would like to be treated. Now, in your effort to live well with the new normal, try making a slight change to that recommendation. Instead, treat people the way *they* want to be treated.

If Grandma or Aunt Sally doesn't like to have her photos uploaded to your page, don't do it. If your dad prefers to meet with you for lunch on Sundays instead of a chatting via a Friday evening Skype call, get yourself to lunch on Sundays. If you have one assistant manager who needs a little one-on-one coaching, map out a few minutes to talk with him in-person. By treating people the way *they* want to be treated, you are not forcing the new normal upon them. They will appreciate your consideration, and your relationships with them will be preserved.

Prioritize In-Person Communication

If you get too caught up in the trappings of the digital age, it can be easy to go for days barely speaking to anyone in the physical world. Leaders aren't the only ones who really need to come out from behind their desks. No matter our professions or interests, all of us can benefit from pushing back from the computer or setting our phones down. Face-to-face communication provides us — and our receivers — the opportunity to use body language and other nonverbal cues in sending and receiving our messages. Our receivers aren't limited to reading between the lines of our emails or texts.

Even at times when an email, phone call, or text message would suffice, meeting up with co-workers, friends, or family in person offers a personal touch. It shows that the other person is worth your time and attention for a one-on-one visit. This strengthens relationships and improves trust.

Regular Detoxing

Following all of the above suggestions still may not be enough to truly win the battle with today's mobile nation. You may need to take extreme measures to protect your offline connections. Your effectiveness and productivity at work, your ability to communicate with fewer misunderstandings, and your psychological health are all on the line. That's why "pulling the plug" on your social media usage is sometimes a practical step. Here are some options for conducting a social media detox:

- If you find yourself juggling multiple accounts, pick one or two social networking tools (for example, Facebook and Twitter), and stick with them only. Gradually cut back on the time you spend on others until you are no longer using them.
- If you spend too much time online, set limits for yourself. Plan 30 minutes or an hour each day to catch up with friends online and update your status. Use a timer. After the time has elapsed, log off and don't return until the next day at the same time.
- If you need a major time-out, choose one day a week (or a full week) to not log on at all. Alert all your close

friends, relatives, and business contacts that you won't be available via social media. If at all possible, challenge yourself to meet everyone face-to-face that day.

Be Mindful

If I can give you one message to take away on this topic, it's that you should think carefully about what you are doing online. Practice some level of mindfulness about your social media use. Be honest with yourself about the impact it has on your daily life. Like many of the other elements of the Turning Point program, this won't be an easy task. But when having real connections as opposed to superficial online friendships is the payoff, the journey is totally worth it.

Aaron Rentfrew

Turning Point: Diet

The Turning Point: Healthy Eating

The typical American diet consists largely of processed foods, artificial flavorings and additives, and an abundance of other unhealthy components, factors that are contributing to the obesity epidemic, according to many experts. New understandings about human dietary needs have inspired a plethora of diets that purport to restore the body's natural processes. But beware: Many of these dietary regimens are restrictive and unbalanced, so while they may help you lose weight in the short term, they cannot support a healthy lifestyle over the long term. That said, the simplicity of a well-balanced natural diet can have profound effects on how your body functions. Before you make a switch, though, you need to know a few things about this dietary change and how it will be part of the Turning Point in your life.

The Problem with Today's Diet

More than 10,000 years ago, humans began using agriculture and animal husbandry to survive. Unfortunately, this departure from nature's intended sources of sustenance has contributed heavily to the widespread occurrence of conditions such as diabetes, obesity, coronary heart disease, atherosclerosis (hardening of the arteries), and hypertension (high blood pressure) — often called "diseases of civilization." The continued genetic modification of our food sources has further tainted the food supply.

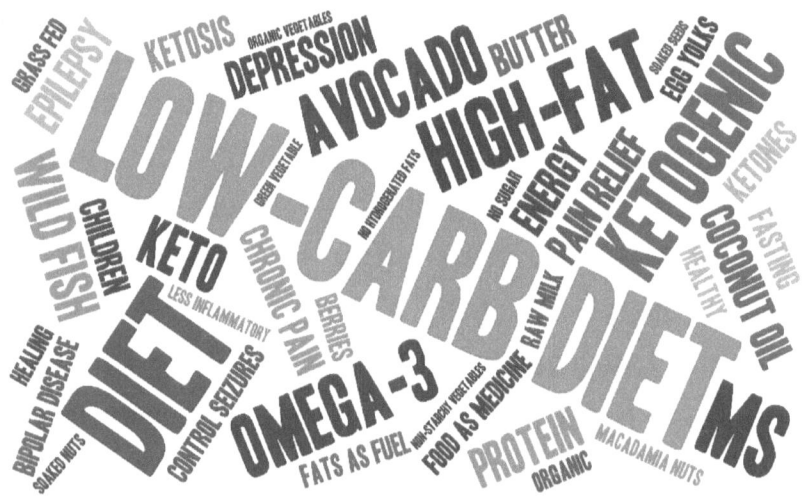

With the advent of the Industrial Revolution, people began to live longer and healthier lives. The world's population began to boom. Wars came and went, medicine grew more advanced, and people got into the rut of instant gratification through TV dinners, fast foods, and myriad other processed foods available at the local grocery store.

What Do Artificial and Processed Foods Do to the Body?

Any food that has been changed from its natural state, which often includes the addition of sodium-containing additives to improve shelf life, is considered to have been processed. Unfortunately, too much sodium is not good for the heart and circulatory system. In his article, "Fast Food Fever: Reviewing the Impacts of the Western Diet on Immunity," Ian Myles explains how the abundance of simple sugars, salts, and saturated fatty acids in the typical Western diet increases inflammation and hampers many of the body's functions. I can tell you that before I changed my eating habits, my body was in pretty bad shape, and I was often in pain.

Unhealthy Fat Synthesis

Both saturated and unsaturated fats affect the cellular membranes throughout the body. The impact on the immune and central nervous system is most dramatic. The immune system functions by essentially eating and digesting harmful bacteria, viruses, and pathogens. Changes in the cellular structure of the immune system lead to a greater risk of infection, inflammation, and illness. An appropriate balance of fats allows brain cells to fire quickly and appropriately. Fat is therefore a necessary factor in health, and cutting out all fat could be catastrophic.

An appropriate combination of healthy fats results in different pathways of digestion and storage. Fats are used by the body's cells to reinvigorate unhealthy tissues and promote stronger immune function. But the synthesis of unhealthy fats, such as those found in many packaged snack foods, transforms them into complex, nearly inaccessible reserves of energy. As a result of these changes in the hydrocarbon chain, the fats become solid and more likely to cause problems in the body. Additionally, an inappropriate combination of fats promotes rapid fat storage within bodily organs and tissues.

What Can You Do?

Our bodies have grown used to the instantly available, savory, flavor-defining profiles of unhealthy fats and salts. Knowing how pervasive processed foods are today, it may seem impractical to try to avoid them and return to the diet of our ancestors. But it's not impossible. If you stop and think about the way our ancestors lived and ate, hunting for fresh foods, gathering nuts and berries, and finding nature's intended sources of sustenance, you'll notice something interesting. All of these foods are still around today. You can find them in the grocery store under labels that say "non-GMO," "organic," and "grass-fed." If you look for these and other hallmarks of non-altered, unprocessed foods, you can start to make healthy dietary changes. The following guide to getting back to the basic eating habits of your ancestors will help.

The Solution

The body needs the right mix of fats, proteins, and carbohydrates to work efficiently and appropriately. However, the modern diet is filled with unhealthy amounts of fats and carbs, and often lacks the best types of protein. For example, Spam is not a good protein. Why? Because it's processed. Obtaining the right combination of foods requires some understanding of healthy fats and how animal proteins differ from plant proteins.

Investigating Healthy Fats

Often, any fat with the term "omega" in the name is thought to be healthy, and this is true to some extent. Each of these fats is needed for proper body functioning. However, only omega-3 and omega-6 fats are essential fatty acids, meaning they must be obtained from food.

Omega-3 Fats

The body uses omega-3 fats to neutralize harmful, nonbound oxygen atoms, also called "free radicals," which can then be excreted from the body. Omega-3 fats have been shown to reduce the risk for cardiovascular disease, improve health, diminish digestive problems, and increase youthfulness.

Omega-6 Fats

Our bodies also need omega-6 fats to function correctly. These fats are a component of high-density lipoproteins, also known as "good cholesterol," and low-density lipoproteins, commonly called "bad cholesterol." The terms "good" and "bad" are somewhat misnomers, since both types of cholesterol are needed to survive. For example, LDL cholesterol includes elements that are essential to the process of activating Vitamin D. However, some omega-6 fats have been linked to increased incidence of inflammation. In addition, according to the University of Maryland Medical Center, there is evidence to implicate them in a condition known as "complex regional pain syndrome."

Omega-9 Fats

Since the body can synthesize omega-9 fats from unsaturated fat, a deficiency of omega-3 fats or omega-6 fats is often accompanied by an increase in omega-9 fats. Omega-9 fats do benefit the body, but you don't need to eat them the way you need to eat omega-3 and omega-6 fats.

The key to getting the utmost benefit from omega-3 and omega-6 fats is balance and ratios, but we'll discuss that more in a minute. First, you need to understand how fats are used in the body.

Metabolism of Healthy Fats: Anatomy of Fat Synthesis

When your body is under stress, such as when you are walking or exercising, the reservoirs of fat stored in your tissues are released. Often, these reservoirs are made up of saturated fatty acids. These types of fats have a straight, chainlike appearance, and compared to unsaturated fats, they have more energy stored in their atomic bonds. This means it takes less saturated fat than unsaturated fat to perform any given action.

Ideally, you should eat to provide your body with the right ratio of fats so that you use the fat you eat as needed rather than storing it in your body long-term. Although some healthy fats may be stored in tissues, the majority are used immediately, and the current prevalence of obesity is due in part to the deficiency of healthy fats in the modern diet.

Fat Ratios

According to the University of Maryland Medical Center and other sources, the typical American diet contains between 14 and 25 times more omega-6 fats than omega-3 fats. In contrast, humans evolved on a diet where the balance of these fats was much closer to 1:1, and numerous studies have shown a decrease in the risk for various diseases when people eat a diet where the ratio of omega-6 fats to omega-3 fats is 5:1 or lower.

Loads of omega-6 fats are probably sitting in your cabinet right now. Do you have a bottle of corn oil or canola oil in your pantry? Those are heavily processed omega-6 fats, which contain elevated levels of linoleic acid. Other processed oils containing unhealthy omega-6 fats include soybean oil, safflower oil, sunflower oil, and cottonseed oil. Look for these in ingredient lists, and avoid them when you can.

Some other foods containing unhealthy amounts of omega-6 fats include:

- Almost any type of fat described as "partially hydrogenated" or "vegetable spread."
- Meats from animals that have been given steroids and/or antibiotics to grow faster. (These meats have poor ratios of omega-3 to omega-6 fats.)
- Imitation butters and margarines.

The linoleic acid in omega-6 fats is not the same thing as alpha-linolenic acid, which is a type of omega-3 fat that can be found in plants. When considering which foods to include in your diet, you'll want to prioritize foods with omega-3 fats and limit those with omega-6 fats in order to bring your fats ratio into a healthier range.

Here's a list of some common foods that contain healthy omega-3 fats:

- Fish, krill, and shrimp. (Wild-caught is almost always better.)
- Unsalted nuts. (Avoid those that are salted, flavored, or processed for long-term storage.)
- Whole, fresh fruits.
- Meats from grass-fed animals and butter from grass-fed cows.
- Green, leafy vegetables.
- Olive oil.
- Flaxseed oil.

It's important to consider processing when choosing healthy sources of fats. If the food item has been processed — canned, made with genetically modified organisms, or otherwise "enhanced,"— it is no longer in its natural state. As a result, its health value is likely to be lower.

Animal Proteins vs. Plant Proteins

Dieticians have argued over the value of animal versus plant proteins in the diet for centuries. One thing we know, though: Our ancestors were not just eating nuts, fruits, and vegetables; they were eating a varied diet of hunted and gathered items. For omnivores — creatures that eat animals and plants — diets without meats often lack essential amino acids. Since amino acids form the building blocks of all the proteins that the body creates, a purely vegetarian diet is limited in its ability to provide nutrition as nature intended.

Animal and plant proteins both provide benefits to the body, and some foods, such as fish, contain higher levels of nutrient-dense proteins and healthy fats. But nowadays, people must be cautious about eating too much fish due to the prevalence of mercury in the world's water-dwelling creatures. Ultimately, the key to figuring out what to eat and what not to eat involves finding nutrient-dense proteins and preparing them in a healthy manner.

The Great Conundrum of Grains

While thinking about the diet of our ancestors, it's easy to get lost in the confusion over grains and berries. Grains can be beneficial to the body, but modern grains are different from the grains that people ate before the development of agriculture. Today's grains, especially refined white grains, are key causes of inflammation. The starch in these foods is quickly metabolized into simple sugars by the enzymes in saliva. Once these sugars enter the bloodstream, if they are not used immediately for energy, they are converted into stored fat. Unfortunately, this process is partially responsible for many ailments, including the following:

- **Hyperglycemia.** This condition of excessively high blood sugar is a precursor to the development of diabetes.
- **Heart disease.** Too many saturated fats and simple sugars in the diet increase LDL cholesterol and triglyceride levels in the blood. Elevated levels of these "bad" forms of cholesterol are associated with hardening of the arteries, inflammation, and high blood pressure.
- **Mental health issues.** Have you ever felt a burst of energy after eating a candy bar? If so, you've experienced a sugar rush, brought on by the brain's

recognition of a sudden supply of energy. However, this sugar rush is generally followed by a rapid drop in blood sugar as the pancreas kicks into overdrive to eliminate the excess glucose from the bloodstream. This can lead to the release of stress hormones and something of a state of shock in the brain. Although the imbalance is short-lived, it can wreak havoc over time, and your mental health will suffer.

Grains are also associated with another condition that seems to be on the upswing: gluten sensitivity. Gluten is a protein found in many common grains, and in people who suffer from gluten intolerance, the digestive system responds to those grains with an immune response that increases the rate of muscle contractions in the digestive tract, causing diarrhea, cramps, discomfort, and of course, inflammation.

Analyzing the Diets

Many different types of diets have been studied and used to fight the so-called "diseases of civilization." Some of the most popular of these diets have been revealed to be nothing more than get-rich-quick schemes, and positive results are few and far between. However, eating plans that focus on restoring the body's natural diet — the diet of our ancestors — often go unnoticed by mainstream media. The Paleo Diet, the Bulletproof Diet, the Primal Blueprint, veganism, and vegetarianism all involve cutting out many sources of simple sugars and restoring the body's natural balance. However, some of these diets are either too strict or too lax to truly provide benefits from inflammation and pain.

To live a truly healthy life, you don't need a diet; you need a permanent change in eating habits — an eating plan that combines the benefits of some of these diets with the facts of science. Although veganism and vegetarianism may be healthy, they are flawed. Many vegetables may be fertilized with chemicals, butter may made with antibiotic-enriched milk, and some modern forms of vegetables do not even resemble what was once a superior source of vitamins and nutrients.

Consider the common carrot. It wasn't always orange! In fact, ancient descriptions of carrots indicate that most were purple or white. There were also red and yellow varieties. Hybridization by farmers over the centuries eventually led to mass cultivation of the now-familiar orange carrot. This may not seem like a genetically modified food, but it is. Like other GMOs, it may not contain all the natural benefits of its ancestral predecessors.

The Turning Point Eating Plan

You might think that embracing the eating habits of your ancestors would be a complex endeavor, but getting started is not really all that complicated. The key is changing how your body processes food. Essentially, once you start eating healthier, unprocessed foods — such as butter from grass-fed cows, meats from wild or grass-fed animals, and nuts — you will balance the ratio of omega-3 to omega-6 fats in your diet.

Why the focus on grass-fed animals? The reason is that meat from animals that graze on grass is physically different than the meat of animals that are given processed feed laden with antibiotics and steroids. Grass-fed animals eat a natural diet, and subsequently, they have a healthier omega-3 to omega-6 fat ratio in their bodies. Furthermore, the antibiotics, steroids, and chemicals in typical cattle feed make their way through to the udders of dairy cows, giving the milk from these animals a less favorable ratio of omega-3 to omega-6 fats.

Start by incorporating more omega-3 fats into your diet, and cut back on your intake of omega-6 fats, such as vegetable and canola oil. Remember, ancestral diets had close to a 1:1 ratio of omega-3 to omega-6 fats.

It takes a little adjustment to make the switch, but once you have shaken your body free from the constraints of a modern diet, your body will start to rely on the food you eat instead of storing it as fat. The key lies in eating the right, nutrient-dense foods just until you feel like you're getting full. Don't take that extra bite, either. Instead, put away the food until you feel hungry again.

Obviously, high-energy lifestyles demand more carbohydrates than more sedentary ones, which is why the Turning Point eating plan is adjustable to meet all types of energy needs. For example:

- **For a high-energy lifestyle:** If you engage in high-energy workouts such as CrossFit at least three to four times per week, be sure to include between 200 and 250 grams of carbs daily.

- **To achieve weight loss:** Limit your carb intake to between 100 and 150 grams per day. However, staying closer to 100 grams will help you lose weight faster.
- **To maintain a healthy body weight:** Once you are at a healthy weight, limit your carb intake to about 150 grams per day to help maintain your weight.

In addition to knowing how many carbs you can eat, you need to know what types of carbs are good and bad. This chart will help you choose wisely.

Good Carbs	Bad Carbs
• Sweet potatoes • Brown rice • Fresh fruits • Raw honey • Berries • Quinoa and chia seeds	• White pasta • Bread • Drinks containing high-fructose corn syrup • Sports drinks and energy drinks • White sugar • Cereals

Making the decision to switch from a modern, not so-healthy diet to the Turning Point eating plan is the hardest step. Once you start changing what you eat and modifying your portion sizes, you will find many that this new way of eating incorporates many of your favorite tastes. In fact, you can find thousands of tasty, simple dishes that align with the principles of the

Turning Point eating plan on the Web at http://thepaleodiet.com/recipes and https://paleomagonline. com/.

For starters, ditch those drinks full of high-fructose corn syrup. Replace solid and heavily processed fats in your kitchen, such as partially hydrogenated vegetable shortening, bottles of vegetable or canola oil, and hydrogenated vegetable oil spreads (often hiding under the label of "butter substitutes") with natural fats such as extra virgin olive oil, coconut oil, and lard, butter, and beef tallow from grass-fed cattle.

You will find that the answers to stopping pain, inflammation, and the diseases of civilization are easy to find in the grocery store, at the farmers market, in the ground, on trees and bushes, in the ocean, in your backyard, and even in your cabinet. You just have to know where to look. Good luck, and if you start to feel down about changing your eating habits, think about this: Adopting *the*

Turning Point eating plan is one of the few ways you can actually relive and connect with what your ancestors did on a daily basis.

The End is the Beginning

So what's your plan now? Are you ready to implement changes in your life that will lead you down the path to change? We all have to make the choice to change at some point. Usually, these types of adjustments are preceded by pain. Pain is after all the best launchpad to growth.

Reading a book and finding a path are great, but without action, I promise you things will remain the same. We invite you to come and interact on our forum with people just like you who are dealing with their past to achieve their goals. As a member of our livingright.co forum you will find a place where you can share your success as well as your failures with those who are looking to reach their full potential.

You never know when you hold the perfect advice or story to motivate and inspire someone unless you are willing to share it.

Helping others will be the cornerstone of your personal growth and dramatically improve your self-worth. A wise man and mentor once told me that "if I want self-esteem, then do esteemable things." This advice changed my life and my approach to my problems. I would implore you to do the same.

Reap the rewards that your stories and experience can bring others. It's a simple solution to closing the circle and maintaining your progress. Reverting to old behaviors becomes less and less likely the more you pour yourself into helping others.

I would also recommend taking a look at "Finding your Prism" to maintaining your growth and launching yourself into peace of mind. It's a great resource for dealing with issues in the moment and harnessing proper perspective.

I look forward to seeing you on our site and hearing your feedback as you progress towards your personal goals. Hearing your story will help me get better as a person and provide follow-ups on the subject matter. I'm always looking for ways to assist others and provide my life experiences as I go. My goal is to create a community of like-minded individuals that are only here to help each other and grow.

Never stop progressing and always look for ways to get better. This guide is a great set of tools to fix your past and put you on a path to health and wellness. But, there are so many other ways to learn and grow. My blog is a great place to start, but I challenge you to find the best path that works for you once you have completed these tasks and utilized the tools in the previous chapters.

Most people you come across are just trying to keep it together. Stop holding onto that feeling that you are somehow "less than."

Explore your capabilities and never give up. You are so much stronger than you realize. This text is just the first step in your journey. The benefits are 100% based on action and execution so don't sell yourself short and take your personal recovery into your own hands.

If there are parts of this book that you would like clarification on feel free to ask for help and send me a direct message. I have no problem talking about ways to make the message work for you, everyone learns in a different manner, and I want to be sure my message can work for you too!

Until we meet again, this is Aaron Rentfrew signing off. Now pick up your paint brush and make a masterpiece!